MY VILLAGE
BY
THE SEA

Dear Billie,
Thank you for your
kind support

      Anastasia.

      11-21-2023

VILMA LIACOURAS CHANTILES

MY VILLAGE
BY
THE SEA

FOLKTALES OF GREECE

PELLA
PELLA PUBLISHING COMPANY, INC.
NEW YORK, NY 10018-6401

MY VILLAGE
BY
THE SEA

Copyright © 1993
by
VILMA LIACOURAS CHANTILES

Drawings by
VILMA LIACOURAS CHANTILES

Library of Congress Catalogue Card No.

ISBN 0-918618-58-4

PRINTED IN THE UNITED STATES OF AMERICA
BY
ATHENS PRINTING COMPANY
337 West 36th Street
New York, NY 10018-6401

For my children
Dean, Jamie, and Maria Nicole

CONTENTS

ACKNOWLEDGMENTS

A gift of the evening quiet when other work was done, this book evolved in mystery. I did not know what I ultimately planned to do, but I loved the tales and their resemblance to Greek village life. It became an adventure. I was deeply moved by "Twelve Months" in 1972 and planned to use the tale as cultural background in a book on Greece I was writing, but ran out of space.

As I reread the stories I translated, I would revise phrases, simplify, rewrite, sigh and dream about this fabled world that reminded me so much of Greece and the people of my nuclear family who were born in Greek villages. Then I would place all the pages I had written in a sea-green folder, now faded and worn, and hide the folder in my desk. This endeavor persisted for years.

I asked teachers and librarians to read some of the tales I had selected. I appreciate the valuable comments of dear friends, Joyce Kildahl and Clarice Wilson, and those of Gay Reetz, Claire Ribaud, and Elizabeth Youman. I acknowledge the inspiration of Greek folklorists, particularly George A. Megas and his vivid interpretation of many of the tales. I am especially grateful to Leandros Papathanasiou, publisher of Pella Publishing Co., Inc., New York, for his interest in publishing this volume as a *collection*. The tales belong together as do families, and are valuable for children and adults to read and enjoy.

PROLOGUE

THESE WONDERFUL TALES, like the sun and sea, belong in our universal village. The folks and animals in the stories, the peoples' pranks and dilemmas, pain and triumph, attitudes to animals, their hopes and feelings are ours, wherever we may live in any culture.

The tales belong together as a classic collection. They depict a wondrous cosmos in which to wander—a simpler, more primitive world that flourished before technology, global communication, and transportation. Often mystical with superstitious and animistic overtones, the world of the tales and the people in them reflect a remarkable dignity despite economic impoverishment. Yet in Greece, and in other countries, that poverty-stricken humanity was also blessed: During centuries of political domination, the Hellenic society in which the tales thrived was gloriously endowed with a culture and tradition.

Folklorists, in fact, link the folk culture from which the tales emerged to antecedents in ancient mythology, literature, and customs. Nicholas Polites, founder of folkloric studies in Greece, advanced the thesis of Hellenic continuity, indicating the link of modern to ancient social customs, folk beliefs, customs of food, shelter, and clothing. Folklorists and anthologists

Stilpon P. Kyriakides and George A. Megas succeeded Polites and perpetuated his theories.

Anthologists usually categorize the stories into four groups: animal myths; tales without magic; tales with magical and supernatural events and characters; and religious plots that may include God, saints, angels, and their miracles. Each group may be subdivided.

The tales of this collection fall into the first three groups: Our Villagers (stories without magic); Our Animals (animal tales); Our Hopes and Dreams (mystical tales with realistic characters). Certainly, the tales can be enjoyed as events of another era. What would we have done in such a situation? Would we have been as fearless, as loyal? And certainly, we can admire the humble family members with remarkable memories. They were responsible for repeating the stories and passing them along to the younger ones.

This tradition can be traced back to Aesop, the witty slave born on the Greek island of Samos in the sixth century B.C. who traveled and told his original tales through Greece and the Middle East. Aesop aimed his wit against tyranny and the baser human traits that he despised. Clearly, the tales of Greece emerged from the generational cycle of an oral tradition. Story-telling was *it* —the cinema, television, and books all rolled into one.

The style of narration—especially the openings and endings—follow a pattern in Greece that continued into the twentieth century. For example, my sister-in-law, Erasmia Simopoulou, of Athens, recalls the way her *yiayia* (grandma) launched a story early in the twentieth century when she was growing up in Arcadia. After announcing the name of the tale, her *yiayia* would repeat a rhyme: *Kokkini klosti demeni / stin anemi tiligmeni/ Dos' tis klotso na girisi/ Paramithi n' arhinisi. Arhi tou paramithiou. Kalispera tis afentias sas. Mia fora kai ena kairo....* (Red thread tied/ to the spinning-wheel/ Give it a kick to spin/ A story to begin. The story begins. Good evening to you. Once upon a time....)

As for the endings, Greek tales usually end with one of the following phrases: "And they lived well and we even better"; "Neither you nor I were there to believe this story"; "And they lived well and not better. I was there and took a walk"; or "I took a walk there and I know." Or the tale may conclude with a couplet:: *K' etrogan k' epinan/ kai psofisan ap' tin pina...* (And they ate and drank/ and died of hunger.)

I became aware of the resemblance between life in a Greek village and episodes depicted in the tales, the humor as well as the pathos. Activities and customs in the stories often mirrored the era of my grandparents' generation that I heard about while growing up. When I visited my father's Messenian and mother's Lakonian birthplaces, I visited village shops like those described in the tales, met people with amazingly similar characteristics, walked along the seaside, picked wild herbs, admired the trees and flowers, especially the spirit of the Hellenes. I was familiar with Greek proverbs and tales at home, had absorbed the customs, knew the strict rules when I misbehaved.

The tenacity of the culture and the passionate feelings of the Hellenes for their family and country are remarkable qualities. These fundamental values are worthy of our attention.

Therefore, "My Village by the Sea" reflects life in a Greek village through the recollections of Dimitri, who describes his family life as a child when he heard the tales. Dimitri's village is a composite of all the villages in Greece I have known, especially of Koroni, in Messenia. May Dimitri and the tales become your friends.

V. L. C.

1

My Village by the Sea

Κάθε τόπος καὶ ζακώνι
Κάθε γειτονιὰ καὶ πράξη.

MY VILLAGE BY THE SEA

ONCE LONG AGO I lived in a fragrant stone hut by the sea. Our hut was painted white. It was topped by a bright red tile roof. Shutters on the windows, carved from an old oak, guarded us from the dazzling sun in summer and gusting winds in winter. But I recall the shutters open wide with warm sunlight streaming into every corner of our home.

Animals lived nearby, part of the household. Roosters and chickens pecked on the thirsty ground around the goats and an old gray donkey. That faithful donkey provided the only form of transport for the family.

Wild dill and thyme, oregano and sage thrived on the hillside, beckoning with their lively scents. We dried herbs for soups and stews. For tummy ailments, we would brew tisanes from aromatic camomile and *tylion* (linden flowers).

In early spring, we picked shoots of wild dandelion, chard, and burdock, which we cooked for dinner. These prized greens were harbingers of home-grown vegetables in summer. Our trees produced the most delicious fruit I have ever tasted. Now I only remember the fruit hanging like gems in the sun, not my fatigue picking the fruit.

This humble dwelling was my haven. My refuge. My sanctuary. Surely it was plain and simple, only one large living room with diminutive partitions around it for the kitchen and bedrooms. But it never seemed meager to me. Even now, more than forty years later, I feel a sense of peace remembering its aromas and sounds.

Our Neighborhood

Other villagers lived around us. We could not see their homes from our door. Like ours, the neighboring homes were nestled among the pines and lofty cypresses. Huts were sprinkled on the hillside all the way down to the *plateia* (village square) at the shoreline.

And beyond the coast drifted the luminous Mediterranean. The sea was truly our universe of wonder, of fear and mystery. It cradled the narrow beach all the way to the medieval fortress at the eastern side of the village and far into the pale horizon.

We walked by the sea after the siesta. When much of the world would be preparing supper between 5 and 6 o'clock, it was only "afternoon" in my village, a time for refreshment and a *volta* (stroll). The favorite adult treat was rich Greek coffee with a pastry and glass of cold water. Then villagers walked from the square to the fortress, relaxing after the work of a long day. Mothers promenaded with their infants. Young people met here, and sweethearts could exchange secret messages with their eyes. So we often called the seaside pathway the *nymphobazari*, the "bridal bazaar." I could never begin to count the hours of my life spent here—as a baby with my mother, as a growing boy playing ball with my friends.

Daily Life in Our Home

Our home overflowed with scents and resounded with clatter. Each season brought new flavors. Everything we needed was in the living room. Solid wooden floors and ceiling beams offered stability. Plaster walls displayed family homespuns and embroideries. Furniture was comfortable: a gracious walnut table and snug chairs where we ate and sang, played games, and heard tales and myths; a cot where I slept as a child; a few extra chairs and small tables. Furnishings were crafted by hand to last forever. The table, created by *papouli* (grandpa) when he was a young man, had acquired a lustrous patina.

In the morning, we greeted each other in this central living room and I kissed my parents and *yiayia* (grandma) and *papouli* here before going to bed. In this room, Athena, my gentle sister, and I heard many tales. The tale would begin with a little poem, and end with a special closing, "... and they lived happily ever after," or "... and they lived well and we even better" or "They lived well. I took a walk there and I know." Characters in the tales became real to me as the villagers of my neighborhood.

Mouth-watering aromas floated around the room: dried herbs; fresh basil on windowsills; vegetables in tomato sauce with garlic, onions, and olive oil; cinnamon, clove, oregano, thyme.

I was born on the cot under the window facing the sea. Yiayia would remind me of my lusty cries at birth. Apple and quince trees were in bloom, she said, and wheat ripened under a warm sun. Neighbors of-

3

fered fruits for good wishes. *Theo Yianni* (Uncle John), mama's brother, had returned home from army duty, and he brought the best treat, *loukoumia* (jellied candies). My birthday became an annual event at home, although namedays were celebrated in most families. Mama, with her brown eyes shining, would make my favorite *karydopita* (walnut cake) on my birthday and offer it with a smile.

This is also the home where papa was born and *papouli,* long before papa. *Yiayia* came here from her village on her wedding day with handwoven coverlets and embroideries she had made herself. When mama married papa, she brought her dowry of linens she had embroidered.

How many times we heard about mama and papa's wedding day! All the villagers joined in the festivities with dancing and singing, eating and drinking. *Yiayia* shook her head and smiled as she described the wedding party that lasted three days. To me, it became yet another radiant fairy tale.

The Seasons

In winter, the rains came. At last, our dry earth was moistened. The rain pattered on the roof like music made by gentle fingers on a harp. Rainwater flowed into a cistern. We used rainwater for our donkey and goats and for plants. But my family drank the fresh, cold water from our well.

How could I ever forget the well? I was elated the first time I was allowed to tug a bucket of water from the dark hole in the ground. Papa helped me.

My arm muscles ached. As I grew older, drawing the well water became my chore. I had to haul water into the kitchen because we did not have running water. It became a vital task.

My heart still pounds remembering songs we sang and card games and backgammon we played, the stories I heard, the sight of a schooner sailing in the distance. I was mystified, gazing through the window. Where was the ship going, I wondered? Where could it be coming from? Will it dock in our village?

The Village Square

Narrow pathways, softened by a blanket of pine needles, led from our door to the square. I would run down the path to school. Often I raced to the quay to meet *Theo Yianni* and his caique. *Papouli* carried roasts to be baked at the *fourno* (oven-bakery).

The village square was the hub of our universe. It was a social and business plaza where the *fourno* and other shops functioned. Those were the years of trades-men and artisans. They worked in their shops: perfecting their craft; selling supplies; fashioning cloth into sails, leather into shoes; grinding flour; mixing sugar, flour, and almonds into pastries. The blacksmith forged iron plates into shoes for horses and mules. People met and gossiped, paused for a drink of water by the spring. Old men dozed on a bench.

My school stood near the square. It was equipped with a wide yard where I played *podosfairo* (soccer) with my friend, Spero, and other classmates.

5

The quay was the most exciting place when *Theo Yianni* and other fishermen unloaded their catch late in the morning.

"Come buy fresh cod and porgy! Red mullets and sardines today! Look at these plump smelts," they would call as we gathered around.

In summer when school closed, *Theo Yianni* would let me help untangle the nets. What a job! I sat on the ground next to him. He told me how the fishermen dragged the huge net filled with fish from the sea. I wanted to go fishing but the boat set sail at dark.

Theo Yianni and I had a secret joke. He would whisper with a grin, "Where's *mangouro-bastouno-klitso-vlaho-koumoutsaros!*" We exploded with laughter, hearing that 14-syllable name of an imaginary man.

In my village, I knew everyone by name. The villagers called me Dimitri. I could tell you where everyone lived—the miller, the baker, *Kyra Fofo* (Mrs. Fofo), the *polylogou* (babbler or chatterbox), and the woman who read fortunes in coffee grounds. Street numbers for homes did not exist. The mailman carried letters to homes, or folks stopped by the small post office in the *plateia* for their mail.

May Day Picnic

Flowers enriched our life, especially on the first of May, when we rested from work. At dawn, we gathered wildflowers: poppies and camomile blossoms and marguerites. Mama shaped a wreath from the stem of a wild olive tree and tied the flowers to the wreath. She hung it on the door or balcony for good luck.

Then off we went for a picnic on the hill. We packed a basket with hard-cooked eggs, cheese and bread, olives and cold meats and fruits and leftover pastries from Easter. Our amusement came from watching golden lights dancing on the sea far below us. Hues mingled magically before our eyes—inky blue-violet in the distance blended with sapphire and indigo. Closer to shore, the sea was clear as an emerald. Suddenly someone would begin singing a folk song and we sang one after another and chattered.

The Harvests

As a child, I never realized how impoverished we were. My parents did not complain. The clothes we wore would seem shabby today. But my knitted sweaters were warm. I was unconcerned that my trousers, clean and warm, were cut from papa's worn pants, or that *Yiayia* would unravel old sweaters and knit new ones from the yarn. I never felt deprived. My friends all dressed the same homely way. When the hand-loomed sheets and towels were frayed in places, mama trimmed and reinforced them or made towels and pillow cases from the sturdy sections of the fabric. Nothing was wasted.

We had enough food. Delicious food. We owned land—our *ktima*—with orchards of olive trees. Our garden flourished with fruit trees and tender vegetables—beans and okra, tomatoes, eggplants and peppers, onions and potatoes. We had goats for milk, from which we made noodles and *trahana* (sour-milk pasta), and cheeses.

When fruit trees ripened—peach and pear and apricot—the picking and eating began. We had an almond tree where *papouli* would sit and pluck on the strings of his guitar. He would sing his favorite folk song about the girl with curly blonde hair who sat under the *amygdalia*. Perhaps he recalled *yiayia* as a maiden; she was the fairest member of the family with sea-blue eyes.

Sour cherries (*vyssina*) ripened in midsummer. Athena and I could climb the tree and pick basketfuls of plump cherries until our fingers turned red from the juice and our muscles were sore. Then mama and *yiayia* would pile the cherries on the table in the garden, and pit them. *Yiayia* washed a hairpin that held her silvery hair in a knot, and with the round end, she popped out the cherry pits. When the cherries were cooked with sugar, the preserves were delicious, my favorite spoon sweet. We stirred some preserves into cold water in summer for the most refreshing drink, *vyssinada*. Then I chewed the cherries at the bottom. Papa tended the peach and fig trees. He would squeeze the fruit to feel if they had ripened. My mouth still yearns for their luscious flavors.

"A tree is known by its fruit," papa would say sternly, watching me from the corner of his eye to see if I heard him. He was a very strict man and I listened to him. I know now what he meant: I should produce good deeds as the tree bears good fruit. But as a child, I was only eager to eat.

Our pomegranate tree was our most amazing tree— an antique, older than *papouli*. Papa hung the pomegranates on a string in the kitchen, and the outer skin gradually dried. But the fruit inside remained fresh. On New Year's Day, *papouli* would throw a pomegranate on the hearth and predict our luck for the year by the number of seeds that spilled out. *Yiayia* squeezed the pomegranates for juice to make a syrup. Whenever I ate the tiny, pulpy red seeds, I thought of Persephone in the ancient myth. She tasted pomegranate after she was abducted. Her mother, Demeter, the goddess of grain, was sad, and winter came to the earth.

Thus I felt enchantment around me, even from sweet basil. Mama planted seeds in pots and cans, and basil grew into immense soft balls, with tiny feathery leaves. When I leaned over to smell the sweet, peppery scent, the basil tickled my nose. *Papouli* would pinch off a sprig of basil and press it into my hand. "It brings good luck," he said gently. I didn't know what to do with the basil he gave me. I did not want to throw it away and invite bad luck, so I tucked the basil in my pocket.

Our olive trees were indispensable. In fact, proverbs expressed their ties to Greek life: "Without olive oil, without vinegar, how can we take a trip?" "Take olive oil from the top and honey from the bottom."

The family picked olives for many days. We would shake the branches until the ripe ones fell. We carried the olives home to cure them. First, we pounded them with a rock or slashed them with a knife. To remove the bitterness, the olives were soaked in water for a week or longer, then marinated with vinegar and herbs. Stored in oil, olives could last for years. We

9

ate olives often. Some olives were pressed for oil. Papa sold the oil and bought our supplies.

Farewell, Village

I prefer to reflect on those happy early years rather than on the sad moments, such as the day we buried *yiayia* in the church cemetery. The village *kambana* tolled mournfully, endlessly, as mourners walked in the funeral procession. Soon after *yiayia* died, *papouli*, too, was laid to rest in the grave next to her.

When I was twelve years old a trauma disrupted my life. That was the day *Theo Yianni* left the village. He had to earn money to send home to his parents and unmarried sisters—mama's family. *Theo Yianni* kissed us goodbye and waved sadly from the road as he walked away from us. He emigrated to America. I became despondent. I lay on my cot and would not eat. My parents had to fetch the doctor from a neighboring town.

The shock of my uncle's farewell launched a harsh awareness: Our future in the village was economically bleak. I vowed I would see my uncle again.

Three years later, I left to find work in America and help my family. I had to go out into the world like the brothers in the tale, "Trak!" When we said goodbye to each other, papa held my hand, mama clung to me. Mama and Athena wept, not knowing if we would ever see each other again. My heart aches when I think of that day. My parents died before I could return to that little hut by the sea.

So I reflect on our joyous moments at the square, the excitement on holidays, our fun playing marbles and kicking a ball around the courtyard. To recapture the innocence of childhood, I think of the tales I heard at home. Our villagers and animals seem to come alive through the characters: Fishermen board their caiques; millers grind the wheat; tavern keepers serve patrons; widows struggle for their children; fathers hope for happy marriages for their daughters; sons must leave home to find work; mothers weep and pray for the children. Thus, I evoke childhood in my village by the sea.

As you begin to read the tales, let me offer to you a sprig of basil as *papouli* had given me for good luck. If you and your family like the tales, read them again and again. The people in them will live forever after. I took a little walk there and I know.

2

Our Villagers

Ἡ φτώχεια θέλει καλοπέραση.

THE CHATTERBOX

ONCE UPON A TIME an old man and a woman lived in our village. They lived in the same little hut for fifty years since the day they were married.

Their names were Pano and Dora. They often called each other "old man" and "old woman" because it was a village custom.

They worked hard for their food, taking care of olive and nut trees in their *ktima*, their family orchard. Beans and tomatoes flourished in their garden. Pano took care of the goat and sheep that produced milk for their cheese. Dora helped Pano collect olives and fruits from the trees. She cooked preserves for their supplies.

In these ways, Pano and Dora were alike. But they were quite different in the way they behaved.

Old Pano was quiet and thoughtful. He could work all day long without talking to anyone. In the forest, he hummed as he chopped wood. He enjoyed listening to the finches chirping in the trees. At night after supper, Pano played the mandolin and sang folk songs. And he liked to join the dancing circle when their friends gathered for a celebration.

Old Dora, however, was a chatterbox, a real prattler. She was known as the village babbler who could not keep secrets. And she was thoughtless. Whatever happened in their home became a story for her to tell.

She would jabber everything to her neighbors. Soon the entire village heard about it!

One morning, old Pano went to the woods to chop wood they needed to cook their food. As he was splitting a log, the earth moved under his feet and he slid into a shallow hole.

Pano was startled. He tried to pull his feet out of the hole. Then he felt something hard under his shoes. He began digging to see what it was. What did he find? A small chest full of gold coins!

"Happy day," chuckled the old man. He was amazed to find such a treasure. He ran his fingers through the gold coins.

Then his smile faded. His brow wrinkled into a frown. He said to himself, "Oh, what shall I do when my wife hears about this? As soon as she learns what I found, she'll babble to everyone!"

Frowning, Pano sat on the root of a tree. He rubbed his brow, closed his eyes, and pondered for a long time.

Then he brightened and looked up. He knew what should be done to solve the problem of Dora's babbling.

Pano put the chest with the gold coins back into the ground where he found it. He carefully covered the hole with soil and leaves.

Returning to the village, old Pano bought a rabbit and a large fish and took them to the woods. He hung the fish from the branch of a pine tree. Then he went to the seaside where his fishing boat was anchored. He placed the rabbit inside his fishing basket and secured the basket between two cane poles.

When he had done all those things, he returned to his hut and quietly said to his wife: "Old woman, I was lucky today!"

"What? What luck did you have, my husband," she asked expectantly. "Tell me. I want to be joyful, too."

"Yes, but please, Dora, *don't* go babble the news to everyone," he implored.

"I promise. I will not tell anyone. I swear by the saint watching us from the icon, I won't tell," the old woman insisted, raising her voice to persuade him.

"Since you gave me your word that you can keep the secret, I'll tell you," said he. "It was like this."

He whispered in her ear, "Today *I found a chest full of gold coins.*"

"Ah! Oh!" gasped old Dora. "Oh! Oh! Oh!" She was speechless for a minute.

Then she flared at old Pano, "Why didn't you bring the chest of gold coins home?"

"I thought it would be better if we go together to dig it up," replied he.

The old woman quickly—very quickly—wrapped her shawl around her shoulders and followed her husband into the woods.

On the way he said calmly, "Do you know what I heard recently? Fish are growing in the woods and animals of the forest live in water."

"What are you saying, silly man? Do you believe those foolish words?" she snapped.

"Don't you believe it, my wife? Come see for yourself."

He took her to the pine tree where he had hung the fish.

Old Dora gaped at the fish dangling from the branch. "Strange!" she cried in disbelief. "How did the fish grow here?"

The old man pretended to be surprised, as if he, too, could not believe what he saw.

"Eh, why do you waste time?" cried Dora. "Climb up and cut the fish. I'll make fish soup for dinner."

The old man climbed the tree and lowered the fish. Then they continued on the road until they came to the seaside. The old man walked ahead of Dora, carrying the fish.

"Something is jumping inside my fishing basket," he remarked. They looked into the basket and found the rabbit.

"So everything you heard was true!" the old lady gasped. At first she was amazed. Then she shrugged and snapped at Pano, "Take the rabbit out of the box. I'll cook *stifado* (rabbit and onion stew) for supper."

The old man carried the rabbit under his arm and they walked toward the woods to find the chest. When he reached the spot where he had buried it, Pano dug down in the earth until he felt the chest. As he opened the lid, his wife's eyes widened like soup bowls. She touched the gold coins and picked up a few, jingling them like a child with a magical toy.

Pano hid the chest under his coat and they returned to their hut. They hid the chest in a secret place where visitors would not see it.

So on that day the old man and the old woman

became very wealthy and began to live a comfortable life. But they did not tell anyone about the treasure.

After some time had passed, the old woman, who could not keep secrets, began changing her life style. She invited neighbors to her home, spending much money on lavish parties and fancy clothes.

The neighbors were surprised to see many imported candies and exotic foods rather than her usual homemade preserves and cakes.

Naturally, Pano was upset by Dora's behavior. "Why are you spending so much money!" he demanded. They began to argue.

"Why scold me?" she cried indignantly. "I have as much right as you have to the gold pieces in the chest!"

When he heard her reply, the old man lost his patience. He realized that if Dora continued to spend money recklessly, in a short time they would be poor again. So he hid the chest with the gold coins where his wife could not find it.

The old woman was furious! She decided what to do. "I'll go to the court to complain," she said to herself.

The judge was well known throughout the village for his fairness.

Standing before the judge in the courtroom, she began, "Judge, your honor, ever since my husband found the chest with the gold coins, he has changed. He has become a different man. He doesn't want to work and he gets drunk. I want you to take the gold coins from him and give them to me. I can manage our money much better than he can."

The judge sent an officer to summon the old man to court and he also asked the village jurors to come to the trial.

So the officer went to the old man's hut as the judge requested. "The judge asked that you bring the gold chest and treasure with you to the courtroom," he told the old man.

"What treasure fiddlesticks and green horses?" bantered Pano to the officers.

"Don't pretend you don't know. Your wife came and complained to the judge. She said that since you found the chest with the gold pieces you have changed. You became like a different person."

What could the old man do! He had to go to court. So he followed the officer into the courtroom. The jurors were seated, waiting for the trial to begin.

The old man looked about the courtroom.

"Have pity on me, good gentlemen. For which treasure have you invited me? It must be one of my wife's fantasies. Everyone knows she is always telling silly stories."

The old woman was very angry to hear her husband say such things about her.

"How dare you speak that way, husband!" she snapped. "I remember everything and I'll tell it in order! First, we went to the woods and we saw a fish hanging from the tree. . . ."

"Fish from the tree?" repeated the judge, chuckling.

"Yes, your honor,. Then we went to the seaside and we found a rabbit in our fishing basket. . . ."

The village jurors all laughed and laughed. They almost choked laughing.

"Go home, my lady," pronounced the judge sternly, "and stop saying silly things."

So the old man kept his treasure because no one believed the old woman again. That is how she learned to think before she spoke and they lived happily ever after and we even better.

THE EGGS

ONCE UPON A TIME a brave captain had a schooner with brilliant blue and white sails. He kept his boat polished as he delivered wheat and olive oil from port to port.

One day he docked in our village and went to a *taverna* to eat because he was hungry. He asked the tavern keeper, "Have you any food for me to eat?"

"I don't, unlucky one! Everything's eaten . . . except, look here," the tavern keeper replied. "I have leftover fried eggs. Would you like them? Shall I serve them to you?"

The captain agreed. He began to eat the eggs. When the captain took a few bites, a sailor rushed into the *taverna*.

"Captain, we must pull up anchor because of the strong winds! A storm is coming," cried the sailor to the captain.

So the captain ran out and left the eggs uneaten on the dish. He climbed aboard the schooner with the sailors. They pulled up the anchors.

But the captain and crew couldn't keep the ship steady in the violent gale. It rocked this way and that way! St. Nicholas[1] helped them, and at last they were able to save the ship from sinking.

[1]St. Nicholas is the patron saint of Greek sailors and they believe he helps them.

Six years passed before the captain again docked in our port. He went to the *taverna* to pay for the eggs. The captain had those eggs on his mind all those years and he remembered his debt.

But when he offered to pay for the fried eggs, the tavern keeper demanded much more. He wanted the captain's schooner in payment! The tavern keeper figured the debt this way:

"Those eggs . . . ," he began in a loud voice, "if the hen sat on them . . . would produce four chickens each— two roosters and two hens."

He calculated how many eggs the chickens would have laid during the six years since the captain had ordered the eggs. "Surely with such a large debt, I should be able to win the ship!" declared the tavern keeper, rolling his eyes. He said that he would take his case to court and demand the ship in payment for the eggs!

The poor captain was very upset by the tavern keeper's plan.

He wandered about the village in a daze, worried and distressed. What could he do? Would he really lose his entire schooner for four eggs? How could he pay this staggering debt? How could he be able to live without his ship?

He slumped into another *taverna*—the one where all the older men sat and gossiped.

A lawyer was there, too. When he noticed the worried captain, he asked him, "What's wrong? Why are you so anxious, captain?"

The captain told the lawyer about the problem

with the other tavern keeper who was trying to win the captain's ship as payment of his debt for the eggs.

"Captain, order a cup of wine for me to drink and stop worrying. Tomorrow I will win back your schooner for you!"

The captain ordered the wine and it was brought at once to the lawyer. The lawyer wrote a petition and took it to the court. The petition stated that he had been appointed lawyer for the captain.

The next day, the sun rose higher and higher in the sky. Nine o'clock came, ten o'clock, eleven, and it was almost noon. Everyone had gathered in the courtroom, but our lawyer did not appear!

A few minutes before noon, along came the lawyer, singing. He entered the courtroom.

"Look here, good lawyer," protested the judge, "we have been waiting for you all morning and we are dying of hunger."

"Och, your honor, don't pick on me, I have enough troubles. Listen to this! Yesterday I bought five kilos[2] of beans. We were eating beans all day, and this morning, we were eating beans for breakfast. In fact, we still had leftovers. So I went into my field to plant them and I just couldn't come here sooner. . . ."

The tavern keeper who was suing the captain to win the schooner heard the lawyer's words. He exclaimed, "But can you plant beans that are already cooked?"

The lawyer turned to him and retorted. "But can chickens be hatched from eggs that are already fried?"

[2]Each kilo equals 2.2 pounds; five kilos equal 11 pounds.

Our lawyer made his point before the judge! He developed his argument about the fried eggs and summed it up.

"Captain, you ate four eggs—four drachmas[3]—and two drachmas for the bread, a total of six drachmas. Give the six drachmas to the tavern keeper so that he can go back to his work!"

The judge agreed with the defense lawyer and the captain kept his schooner.

As an additional reward, the captain paid the tavern keeper to serve the lawyer as long as the barrel held wine.

Then the captain returned to his schooner, which he kept polished and painted as he sailed from port to port.

[3]Drachmas are currency in Greece. At the time of this tale, each drachma was worth about one cent; four drachmas were about four cents.

ELIA

ONCE UPON A TIME a man called Elia took his wheat
to the village mill to be ground into flour. The next
day, Elia wanted to pick up the wheat flour. He mounted
his mule and set out for the mill.

When he was returning home with the flour, Elia
stopped along the road. He unloaded the mule and
allowed it to graze. As the mule was grazing, Elia fell
asleep on the grass with his straw hat on his head.

Another man rode by on a donkey. The donkey
carried a load of corn fodder. When he saw Elia sleeping, the man took Elia's flour and packed it on the
mule. He substituted in its place his own donkey with
the corn fodder. Then he removed Elia's straw hat
and replaced it with his own cap. The man pulled off
Elia's shoes and placed his own *tsarouhia*[1] on Elia's
feet, took the mule with the flour and went on his way.

Suddenly Elia opened his eyes. He looked around
for his mule but saw a donkey. He opened the sacks
but found only corn fodder. He was puzzled.

Elia stretched his hand to scratch his head but
touched a cap instead of his straw hat. He looked down
at his feet and saw *tsarouhia*.

[1]*Tsarouhia* are leather slippers with large pompons,
which are traditionally part of the evzone costume. In some
Greek provinces, many years ago, *tsarouhia* were worn as
shoes.

"Hey," he cried, "I am not Elia! I had a mule, wheat flour, a straw hat, and black shoes."

He hurried home to Anna, his wife, calling. "Elia, Elia! Where is Elia?"

"He went to the mill," answered Anna.

"What animal did he have?"

"A mule."

"What load did the mule have?"

"Wheat flour."

It was dark but his wife recognized Elia's voice.

"What is wrong, my husband? Come in."

"No, I'm not Elia. I wasn't wearing *tsarouhia*, I did not have a donkey with corn fodder."

His wife opened the door for him and Elia went in, and they stayed well and we even better.

TAKI AND THE THOUSAND GOLD COINS

ONCE THERE WAS a man called Taki who was very poor but happy. He worked hard with his wife all day long to raise enough food to feed their five children.

Every night when they were very tired, they ate their dinner quietly. Then Taki would play his lyre and relax. The children sang folk songs and danced in a circle around the room. The family lived a charmed life that way, working all day and having fun in the evening.

Next door lived a rich man. Every night when he heard the laughter and joyous sounds from the poor man's home, he was very surprised. "How come I am not happy and contented as my neighbor. He works hard all day and enjoys every evening!" So the rich man said, "I'll give him some gold coins and see what he does with them."

So he went to Taki and said, "Because you are an honest man, here, take a thousand gold coins. Open any kind of shop you would like. If you become rich, you can give me back my thousand gold coins or not. These are a gift from me."

All the next day, the poor man thought and thought about what he would do with the gold coins. He took them here and took them there.

"Shall I open a shop? Shall I invest the money? Shall I put the gold coins in the bank and collect the interest? Shall I buy a new orchard? Shall I grow more crops?" Such questions raced through his mind and he could not think of anything else.

Night came and Taki had not worked all day. He had not even earned a dime. His children couldn't say a word. If they laughed, he scolded them.

When he went to bed, Taki was unable to sleep. He was so troubled by the gold coins, he tossed and turned all night. The next day, he didn't go to work, he didn't go anywhere. He just sat and worried and sighed.

His wife asked Taki what was wrong with him. She tried to amuse him and make him laugh. But he turned on her and flared, "Go away."

The next night, the rich neighbor passed by. He walked by another night, and a third . . . but he heard no music from the lyre, no singing by the children, or laughter.

The next morning, he saw Taki coming toward him.

Taki said, "Here, good neighbor, take your gold coins. I don't want them or their troubles."

Since then, Taki and his family are happy in their home, working hard all day and playing his lyre and singing at night. His children dance as they had danced and they are contented again.

THE THREE GOOD TIPS

ONCE UPON A TIME in our village there was a very poor man called Yianni. He had a good wife and a son who was ten years old. Yianni was known as a very honest man who never complained. He worked very hard to make a living, but earned hardly any money and could barely feed himself, his wife and son. In fact, the family had only enough money for their bread.

One day Yianni sadly turned to his wife and said, "My wife, I cannot bear this life any longer. You see me work like a mule from morning until night, and I have nothing to show for my struggle. I do not want to, but I must leave and go to a faraway place and find better work and send money to you and our son or we will starve to death."

"Do as you think best," replied his wife sadly, knowing Yianni had no other choice. "*Sto kalo*, have a good trip, my husband."

So Yianni said goodbye to his wife and son. He went to this place and that place looking for work until he reached a large city. He searched everywhere, but could not find work because he had no trade. So he became the servant of a very rich man.

Yianni worked hard. His employer never paid him for his work. not even a drachma. But the rich man's wife felt sorry for the poor man. Once in awhile she offered Yianni a little money that he would send home to his wife and son.

Then years passed and Yianni became weary of the strange city. He wanted to return to his wife and son because he missed them and our village.

So he packed his belongings and asked the wealthy employer to pay him all the money he had earned.

"Very well, Yianni," said the rich man. "Take your wages." Here!" From his coin bag, the rich employer removed three gold coins and gave them to Yianni.

"Take these three gold coins, Yianni. This is what you earned for the ten years you worked for me. Have a good trip."

Poor Yianni took the three gold coins, knowing they were very low earnings for ten years of hard work, but he said nothing. He sighed and said goodbye to his employer.

As soon as he began walking away, his employer called him back and said, "Give me one gold coin, Yianni, and I will give you a good tip."

"But, sir, ..."

"No, give it to me," interrupted the employer. "It will help you very much."

What could he do? Yianni gave the coin.

His employer said, *"Don't ask about anything that does not concern you."*

Yianni turned away very sadly, because he had given a gold coin.

He had not quite reached the door when the employer called him back again.

"Come here, Yianni, come here! Give me one more gold coin, so that I will give you one more tip."

Yianni gave one more gold coin to the rich man.

"Never leave the road when you begin a journey."

Yianni moved toward the door, worried and thinking to himself, "How can I return to my wife after ten years with only one gold coin from the big city?"

He had hardly stepped from the house when the employer again called him for the third time, "Give me the other coin so I'll give you another good tip."

He took the last gold coin from Yianni and said, *"Control your evening anger at night until the next morning."*

So Yianni left his employer's house with empty pockets and began his long trip home.

On the road, he saw a man high on a tree, hanging gold coins on the branches. This seemed like a very strange act for someone to be doing, but Yianni said nothing, because he remembered the first tip from his employer. *"Don't ask about anything that does not concern you."* He continued walking.

"O-reh, wait!" cried the man on the tree.

Yianni stopped and looked up, frightened by the call. The man told Yianni, "I have been sitting here on this tree for a hundred years, doing the same thing you saw me doing. Many, many people have passed by and all stood here and asked me why I was putting gold coins on the leaves, and I ate them all. Only you did not ask me, but continued on your journey. Bravo! A very wise man are you! Bravo! I shall give you all these gold coins, because you are worthy of them. Take them. You deserve them. *Sto kalo*."

Yianni gladly took the gold coins. He filled his coat pockets, his breast pockets, inside his shirt, and pants pockets, and he continued, happily, on his journey. On the way, he thought, "Really, it was worth one gold coin for my employer's first tip."

After walking for three days, Yianni met some guides leading mules with very heavy loads on their backs. They were traveling in the same direction as Yianni. Yianni asked them, "Please, may I ride on a mule, because I am very tired?" They agreed, and so they continued together on the trip.

After some time, they came to a *taverna* and the guides wanted to drink a little wine. They invited Yianni to join them. Then Yianni remembered the second tip of the employer, "*Never leave the road when you begin a journey.*" Yianni declined the invitation.

"I have enough to eat and drink. I won't drink any wine now," said Yianni.

"Well, if you don't want some wine, will you watch the mules so that we can have a drink?" they asked Yianni.

So the guides entered the *taverna* and Yianni stood in the road and kept the mules from wandering away. As the guides were drinking in the tavern, suddenly there was a shocking earthquake. The ground shook so violently that the tavern was devastated, crushing the tavern keeper and all the patrons, including the guides!

Yianni was startled by the earthquake, but he was not hurt. He crossed himself and thought, "The second tip was also worth one gold coin!"

So Yianni took the mules, packed with olive oil, wheat, and rugs, and he continued his journey home.

After traveling a few more days, at last Yianni arrived in his village and went directly to his home, leading the mules. He knocked on the door, and his wife opened the door. Yianni said, "Good evening."

His wife greeted him, but did not recognize him, and Yianni became very angry. But he remembered the third tip of his employer, "*Control your evening anger at night until the next morning.*" Yianni kept his temper. So he asked his wife if he and his mules could spend the night.

She showed him the stable and said, "I do not allow strange men to stay in my home, but you may spread your blankets here under the loft and sleep tonight."

As Yianni prepared the mules for their rest, he noticed a man pass by and enter the house.

"Aha, my wife must have married again and forgotten about me!"

Yianni was furious. He picked up his gun, and wanted to go in and shoot both of them! But suddenly he remembered the third tip of his employer, "*Control your evening anger at night until the next morning.*" He put the gun away, but he was too troubled to sleep and could not even close his eyes.

In the morning, when Yianni went to feed barley to the mules, he heard the man who had gone into the house say, "I am going, Mother, and at noon, I will send green beans for you to cook."

When he heard his son speaking to his wife, Yianni was astounded and hit his own head with his hands. "To think I had wanted to shoot my own son in anger!" he thought to himself.

Yianni ran into the house and told his wife and son who he was. His wife and son were very happy that he was home again and they hugged and kissed each other.

Yianni and his son unloaded the mules. And with all the gold coins that Yianni brought home, they lived happily ever after and we even better.

3

Our Animals

Ὁ λύκος πρόβατο δὲν γίνεται.

HARRY THE DONKEY

ONCE THERE WAS a chubby donkey grazing in our valley. A fox saw him and wanted to eat him. She went to the wolf and said, "Come and see, wolf, a plump donkey! What a dinner he'll make!"

Off went the wolf with him. When he saw the donkey, sure enough, he began smacking his lips.

"Do you know what we should do, wolf?" cried Mrs. Fox.

"What? You have a good head on your shoulders," replied the wolf.

"Let's buy a boat and load it with olives, and take the donkey with us as our sailor. And when we reach the deep ocean, we can eat him," said the fox. "Come along. You get a boat and I'll go make arrangements with the donkey."

So the wolf went and bought a boat (what a story this is!) and he loaded it with olives.

The fox went straight to Harry the donkey and brought him to the dock and they boarded the boat.

When they reached the deep ocean, the fox said, "Good! Now we are traveling and we don't know if we'll arrive safely. For good or bad, let's make our confessions."

The wolf pretended to be very serious and turned to the fox.

"What sins have you committed? Mrs. Fox."

The fox rocked her head from side to side and confessed, "I stole a few chickens and ate some wild animals—rabbits, geese, hares. Yes, such things I choked and ate."

"You did your job, Mrs. Fox. You ate worms of the earth. Come now and hear my confession."

"Tell me, what sins did you commit?" asked the fox.

The wolf thought for a minute and confessed with a grin, "I ate quite a few sheep, several goats, some calves."

"Oh, little things. Worms of the earth," cried the fox.

Then the wolf turned to Harry the donkey. "Come now, Mr. Donkey, and tell us what sins you committed."

"One day," replied Harry the donkey, "when I carried a load of lettuces on my back, I turned and ate one leaf because I craved it. That's what I did—I ate the lettuce leaf."

"Aha, Mr. Donkey," the fox and wolf shrieked: *You ate lettuce without vinegar, without oil? What a slip! How have we managed to escape from drowning on this trip!* Your sin is very great and we have to eat you!"

Harry the donkey was shocked to find himself suddenly in such trouble. He looked at them and scowled, "Oh, what's going on here. Give me a break!"

"No. We have to eat you," shouted the wolf and fox.

"Alright then," agreed Harry the donkey, "except, listen. When my father died, he gave me a secret message and I have it here on my shoe. Come, Mr. Wolf, read it to me so that I will know what is written, then eat me."

He lifted his rear foot for the wolf to see the shoe. As the wolf bent down to read the message, Harry the donkey gave him a swift kick in the chin. The wolf fell overboard into the ocean.

When the fox saw what happened to the wolf, she jumped into the water to escape. The fox and the wolf both drowned, and that's how the boat and all the olives were left for Harry the donkey . . .

THE CAT, THE LION, AND MAN

ONCE UPON A TIME a cat began to walk around a mountain. As she walked along, she saw a lion on the path in front of her.

The cat quickly crawled into a cave, hoping the lion would stroll away. But the lion had smelled the cat. He moved closer, sniffing and sniffing, until he found the cat.

He said to the cat, "You are like my family but very much smaller!"

The cat promptly replied, "If you lived near Man, you would be small, too."

"But why?" asked the lion. "What is Man?" Is he so large and so wild? Where is he? I want to see him myself!"

The cat offered, "Come with me and I'll show you."

They walked along until they saw a man chopping wood.

"There is Man," whispered the cat, hiding safely behind a tree.

The lion moved closer to the man. "Good morning," he called. "Are you Man?"

"I!" replied the Man boastfully. He held a pickax.

The lion said, "I have heard that you are very strong and I came to fight with you."

"Very well, let's fight," agreed Man. "But first,

help me finish splitting this wood, and then we will fight."

"I will help you," offered the lion.

"Put your paw here in the crack," requested Man, holding open one side of the wood.

The lion placed his paw in the crack of the wood. Instantly, Man released the side of the wood he held. It sprang back and clamped tightly over the lion's paw! The lion howled with pain.

Then Man lifted a club, swung it high, and began lashing the lion, again and again. He almost killed the lion with the beating. The aches and pains! Then he released the lion's paw from the wood.

The lion fell to the ground. He was almost dead.

After awhile, Man loaded the wood on his back, took his pickax and walked away.

The cat crept out of her hiding place and found the lion motionless on the ground. The cat shook the lion, but the lion did not move.

"Can you hear me, lion?" the cat asked gently. "How does Man seem to you?"

The lion moaned faintly.

The cat waited. Some time passed. Then the lion whispered, "If I were a cat, I would become even smaller than you!"

THE HARVEST RACE

ONCE UPON A TIME a fox and a crab met in a meadow. The fox was called Alepou and the crab Marigo. They became friends. One day Alepou and Marigo decided to plant their wheat together in a nearby field. So they did.

In June the wheat ripened. Alepou and Marigo went to the field to harvest the grain.

As they began working, Alepou pretended she was tired and began planning how she could avoid the harvesting. She thought of a sneaky trick to fool the crab. "Marigo, you harvest the wheat. I will go and hold that large rock and keep it from falling and crushing us."

The crab turned and saw a huge rock near the field. Believing the fox, she answered, "Go, Alepou, and hold up the rock, and I will harvest your part of the wheat, too."

This is exactly what the fox wanted to hear! She desired rest while her friend did all the work. Alepou fell asleep while her friend harvested the wheat by herself. In the evening, tired and hungry, Marigo returned home.

When it was time to thresh the grain, Alepou again planned a sneaky trick. She pretended she was sick. So again, Marigo had to do all the work. Marigo threshed the wheat, winnowed the grain, and separated the grain from the hay.

At last the time came when the friends would divide the grain. Certainly Alepou came very eagerly.

The friends piled the grain on one side and made another very large pile of hay. Meanwhile, Alepou plotted how to outwit Marigo. Of course, she wanted to take all the grain and leave the hay for Marigo.

So Alepou said very quickly, "Marigo, I think that I should take the *small* pile of wheat and you should have the *large* pile of hay, or *you* should take the hay and *I* the grain."

But Marigo heard the confusing words and realized the fox was trying to fool her. She said, "Not like that, Alepou. Here's what I suggest. We should go far back, away from the piles of grain and hay. Then we should run, and whoever arrives first wins the wheat."

Ah, how happy the fox was to hear those words! Anyone would like such an easy contest!

So they moved far away from the wheat, and the fox said to the crab, "You start first, Marigo, because I run very fast."

"No, Alepou, I cannot do that. For a fair race, we must begin together," replied the crab.

Just as they began running, the crab caught Alepou's tail and held on tightly. Alepou ran quickly. As she reached the wheat, Marigo fell onto the pile of grain and closed her eyes.

Alepou did not realize what had happened. She waited and waited for the crab to arrive.

After a while, she looked around and saw the crab sleeping on the grain. Alepou cried out in surprise, "Oh, are you here, Marigo?"

"I am here," replied the crab. "I've been waiting for so long, I took a nap."

That is how Crab Marigo—who did all the harvesting and threshing—earned the grain, and Fox Alepou got the hay!

MOTHER OWL AND MOTHER PARTRIDGE

ONE DAY all the birds had a meeting and decided that their children should go to school to learn to read and write. So they found a teacher and appointed him. The school opened and the birds took their youngsters to school and enrolled them.

After a few days, some of the children did not know their lessons in school. The teacher punished them by not allowing them to go home for lunch. They had to stay in school.

Mother Owl's child was among the students who were punished. When Mother Owl noticed children coming home and her child was not with them, she took some lunch for her child.

As she walked along the road to the school, Mother Partridge caught up with her. Her child was also being punished and she, too, was carrying some lunch to her child.

Mother Partridge said to Mother Owl: "Be well, neighbor. I have much work to do. Please, will you take this lunch to my child in school?"

"I will, good neighbor," replied Mother Owl, "but I don't know which of the children is yours."

"Oh," exclaimed Mother Partridge, "that is an easy problem to solve. My child is the most beautiful child in the school!"

Mother Owl went to the school. She asked the

teacher permission to give her child the sandwich she had brought. Then she asked the teacher if she could look at all the other bird children. She looked and looked and looked, but she couldn't find the child of Mother Partridge.

Returning home, she found Mother Partridge and gave back the lunch and said, "What can I do! I looked at all the children for an hour and I couldn't find your child, because there is no more beautiful child in school than mine!"

MAGGIE AND HOOP

ONE DAY a magpie named Maggie perched on a tree in a garden in our village. She had shiny black feathers, a loud voice, and a very healthy appetite.

Maggie watched the pigeons swoop down from their nests in the tree and eat corn. Another day, Maggie saw theim again. Every day she noticed how the pigeons enjoyed their life.

Maggie became very disturbed watching the pigeons having so much fun eating corn. She sighed with envy.

In another tree nearby sat Hoop, a hoopoe with a curved beak and large crown on his head. Hoop the hoopoe heard Maggie sighing and he asked what was wrong.

Maggie flared, "What? When I see how the pigeons live, I get so angry. *What's wrong!* They are much better off than I am! They find their food all ready to eat, and I have to work all day hunting for food and I still go hungry. That's what's wrong!"

Hoop the hoopoe said to Maggie: "You worry yourself over such a thing? It's easy for you to live like a pigeon."

"Really?" asked Maggie. "How?"

"How?" replied Hoop the hoopoe, "I'll tell you. See the pigeons? They are all covered with white feathers. Go and paint your wings white and then slip in among the pigeons. No one will recognize you and you'll live as well as the pigeons!"

"What a great idea, neighbor," cried Maggie the magpie. "They're right when they say 'A neighbor is a blessing.' I'll go now and do exactly as you suggested."

So Maggie the magpie flew nonstop from the tree to the river. There she saw a water mill with a long trench filled with water. She splashed around in the trench until her feathers were very wet.

Maggie noticed the window of the mill was open. Nobody was inside the mill so she entered through the window. Maggie rolled about in the large box of flour until she was all white—as white as the pigeons.

She flew out of the mill directly to the house with the garden where all the pigeons had built their nests. Maggie mingled with the pigeons and began to eat corn with them. For a few days Maggie enjoyed her delightful life with the pigeons.

But one day, the owner of the house brought guests home for dinner. He asked his wife to cook five or six large pigeons for dinner.

His wife caught the largest she could find. Among them was Maggie the magpie. The wife slaughtered the pigeons one at a time and gave them to her daughter to pluck their feathers.

Just as she caught Maggie the magpie, the bird began to scream and caw in the noisy magpie way. The wife was startled by the screeching.

"Why this isn't a pigeon!" she exclaimed, looking at Maggie carefully. The wife was furious! She yanked off one of Maggie's wings and threw the bird out of the garden over the fence into a meadow.

Maggie lay there for a long time. When she recovered, Maggie sat up and said, "God saved me. Such a charmed life as the pigeons have, I can do without! Who needs that kind of a life!"

At that moment, Hoop the hoopoe was sitting in the same tree in the garden and heard Maggie's voice.

Hoop asked her: "What's wrong, neighbor? Nothing but fun and a good time all day long, eh? The rest of us can just go and die! Right?"

When Maggie heard Hoop the hoopoe, she cried: "Oh, go away from here, you horrible hoopoe—you and your suggestions! Only because of you, I got into the mess I'm in. Look at me with only one wing! If I could fly, I'd come up there and beat you to pieces!"

When Hoop the hoopoe heard the angry cries from Maggie, he flew away. Since then he became Maggie's enemy. Whenever he came near Maggie, she would screech for all the birds to help her, and they chased him away. But Hoop the hoopoe knew he was unwanted, and he would fly away like the wind.

THE WOODCUTTER AND THE LION

ONCE THERE WAS an old woodcutter with a very large family. He would take his donkey into the woods daily to chop wood to sell and raise money for his children's food. With his ax, the old woodcutter chopped here and he chopped there as much as he could.

One day a lion appeared where the old woodcutter was chopping in the forest.

"Sit and rest, uncle," the lion told the old man. "I will chop the wood for you. Then you can sell the wood and buy food for your children to eat."

That is how it happened. The old man sat down to rest. The lion cut the wood. The old man loaded it on his donkey and went home with all the wood.

After a few days, the old man again went into the woods. The lion saw him and said, "Bring your donkey every day, old man, so that I can load it with wood for you."

One day in the forest, the weather was terribly hot—hotter than ever. The lion grew so tired chopping wood, he cried, "Sit down, old man, under the olive tree that is very shady and cool so that I can come and rest my head on your knee for awhile."

The lion rested his head on the old man's knee and asked, "Am I handsome, uncle?"

"You are handsome, my son," replied the old man.

"Am I strong and brave?'"

"You are, my lion, you are."

"Am I also intelligent?"

"You are," the old man answered.

"See what a fine youth I am? I have all the charms!" cried the happy lion.

"You have all the good qualities and charms, but you also have a very bad one," remarked the old man. "Your mouth smells!"

The lion immediately stood up, loaded the wood on the donkey and said to the old man, "Come now, take your ax and give me one blow on my back."

"Never will I do such a thing, my son, and strike my friend that has done so much good for me," responded the old man.

"But I wish it," cried the lion, and the old man gave him one blow with his ax and cut open a wound two fingers deep . . .

The old man went again every day to the woods and the lion, wounded as he was, cut wood, and the old man loaded the donkey.

After many weeks passed, the lion said to him, "Look, old man, how does my back appear to you?"

"It is completely well, my good son!" replied the old man.

"The terrible wound healed," agreed the lion, "but the words that you told me—that my mouth smells—hurt me deeply and will never go away. Don't ever come back again to the woods or I will eat you!"

That is why it is said:

A cut of the knife will soon heal away,
But unkind words will hurt and stay.

HERO THE CAT

ONCE THERE WAS a father with three sons. The father became very sick. He thought he would soon die and called his children to give them his last blessing in the custom of our village. He told his sons what he would bequeath to them: To the oldest son, he left a mill; to the middle son, a horse; and to his youngest son, Hero the cat.

Villagers took their grain to the mill to be ground into flour so the oldest son could earn his living. The second son could use his horse to carry loads from village to village to earn his living. Only the youngest son didn't know what job he could do with the cat to earn a living.

The cat observed his young master worried and complaining and asked him: "My master, why are you always worrying and complaining?"

"Why shouldn't I be worried? My older brother has a mill. People take grain to the mill and he grinds it into flour and earns his bread. My other brother has a horse to carry loads from village to village and he earns enough for his bread. What can I do with you, a cat?"

"Don't be angry, my master. You'll see many good things coming from me," replied Hero the cat. (The master laughed to himself.)

"What good will I see from you, you poor cat! I also need to feed you, and that takes money."

"I'm telling you," insisted Hero the cat, "you'll see many good deeds from me. Just make a bag for my shoulder and fill it with grain, and give me a shuttle and iron shoes."

Hero the cat put the iron shoes on his feet, slung the bag with grain over his shoulder, took the shuttle and walked away.

He traveled and traveled until he reached the high mountain in the cool forest where many birds had built their nests. He tossed grain on the ground and the birds flew down to eat and Hero the cat caught them. When he had captured many birds, he took them to the king and said, "My beloved king, you have good wishes and greetings from my master."

Again the next day, Hero the cat put the iron shoes on his feet, slung the bag with grain over his shoulder, took the shuttle and went off to the mountain where many birds nested. He threw grain and birds fluttered down to eat the grain and Hero the cat seized them. When he had caught many birds, he took them to the king as a gift from his master.

Hero the cat continued to catch birds many times until one day the king said to his servants, "When someone again offers the birds, I want to see him. Bring him to me."

The next day, when Hero the cat again offered birds to the king, the servants presented him to the king in the throne room.

"My esteemed king," cried Hero the cat, "here are

the birds from my master to you and he sends you his greetings."

The king told Hero the cat he wanted to visit his master in his home to thank him for all the birds he had sent.

"With pleasure," exclaimed Hero the cat, and pointed in the direction of his master's palace.

Returning home, Hero the cat stopped by the palace of the dragon and entered through a window.

The dragon was entertaining himself, changing himself into different animals. He became a lion, then changed himself into a monkey, a deer, and then a fox. The cat laughed and laughed, clapping his hands at the spectacle. And the dragon was very pleased with himself because the cat was impressed by his talents. He was very flattered by all the attention.

"Bravo, great dragon, you have changed yourself into so many large beasts. Can't you become a really small creature as well?" cried Hero the cat.

"Whatever you wish," replied the dragon.

"Something like a little mouse!" asked Hero the cat.

"I will!" agreed the dragon.

The dragon changed himself into a little mouse, and Hero the cat swallowed him with one *gulp*, and walked away quite happy.

Hero the cat returned home to his master and said, "The king thanks you for all the birds you sent to him and he wants to visit you in person."

"What? The king is coming to my humble little hut?" cried the master. "But I don't have a drachma to my name!"

"Don't worry, my master," reassured Hero the cat. "I've arranged everything. Come. Let me take you to the palace of the dragon, who turned into a mouse and I gulped him down."

Off they marched, Hero the cat, leading his young master to the palace of the dragon.

Hero's master found himself dressed in handsome robes like a prince. He was surrounded by golden rooms lined with large mirrors. All around him, he observed silk draperies on the windows, colorful carpets on the floors, servants with folded arms waiting for orders from him. He thought he was dreaming.

Hero the cat said, "Didn't I tell you, my master, that you would see many good deeds from me?"

That evening, the king arrived. He was very impressed by the palace, which was larger and more beautiful than his own. He asked if the young master would marry his only daughter.

The wedding lasted for forty days and forty nights and Hero the cat lived with them in the palace. Everyone respected Hero the cat. When he died, they placed him in a gold box, and with a splendid ceremony buried him in the palace garden. I was there wearing red trousers.

FATHER PONTIKOS AND DIONE

ONCE UPON A TIME there was a Father Mouse called Pontikos who had a very gentle daughter named Dione. Father Pontikos hoped to find a good husband for her. But he did not want her to marry a mouse!

As he thought about his daughter, Father Pontikos wondered who might be a good husband for her. Then he looked up at the sky. The sun was shining brightly.

"Aha!" he cried. "The sun would make a fine husband for my daughter!" Without losing a moment, he took Dione and traveled to the sun's palace.

Pontikos asked, "Sun, will you take my daughter for your wife? I don't want to give such a wonderful daughter to anyone but you—you who are so strong! You are the strongest in the world!"

"Oh no," responded the sun, shaking his head. "I am not the strongest in the world, as you believe. Look over there at the Clouds. If they cover me, I cannot shine at all, and there is nothing I can do to stop them. Run along to the Clouds. No doubt, you will succeed."

What could Father Mouse do? He journeyed to the Clouds and asked if they would have his daughter for a wife.

"We are not the strongest in the world," laughed the Clouds. "Do you know the North Wind? Well, when the North Wind blows, we are scattered in the sky—and we are lost! Run along to find the powerful North Wind."

So off ran Father Mouse with Dione to find the North Wind and ask him the same question.

"Gladly, dear Father Pontikos," called the North Wind, "I would take your fine daughter to be my wife. But I am not the strongest, as you have been told. Do you see that rugged stone Fortress over there? I have been blowing on it for forty years but have not been able to blow it down!"

Without taking too many words to tell you this story, Father Pontikos ran to the Fortress and offered his daughter in marriage.

The Fortress answered very sadly. "Father Pontikos, do you hear that rumbling inside my walls? Can you guess what makes that noise? *Brave, strong giants—mice.* Yes, mice have been biting at my walls and are almost ready to knock me down! There are no stronger, fiercer, braver creatures in the world than mice and never listen to anyone who tells you otherwise!"

When Father Pontikos heard those words, he was very happy. So he was quite contented when Dione married a strong young Mouse.

KING LION AND THE SLY FOX

LONG AGO in the early years, the animals gathered together and had a meeting to select a king.

They agreed that the bravest and strongest animal was the *lion.* The lion would become their king. So they put a crown on the lion's head and crowned him king of the animals.

After many years, the lion became very sick. The animals went to visit king lion where he lay in his bed.

One day the wolf—a very white wolf—was also going to visit the lion. On his way, he met the fox on the road and said to her, "Fox, come along, so that we can see how our sick king is doing."

"Go as you wish," replied the fox. "Maybe he is even better off than I am. Why should I go to him? Let him come to me!"

The wolf did not answer her. Secretly, he was glad that he could go and tattle to the lion, "The fox said this and that about you." Then the wolf would seem much better than the fox by comparison.

The wolf continued on his way. Meanwhile, the fox very slowly walked behind the wolf to see what would happen when the wolf visited the lion.

The wolf entered king lion's home and sat near the sick lion. The fox hid behind a curtain and listened to them.

Later, the lion commented to the wolf, "That fox

really has been very thoughtless not to say, 'The king is sick and I will go visit him to see how he feels.' "

The wolf replied loudly, "May you live many good years, my king. As I was coming to see you, I saw the fox and told her, 'Let's go to our king to see how he is,' and the fox said, 'I won't go! Maybe he is better off than I am.' "

At that very moment, the sly fox entered the room and bowed low before the king.

"Fox," the king exclaimed, "where have you been all this time and why haven't you come to see me?"

"Oh, my king," replied the fox, "you don't know where I have been! I heard that you were sick, and I asked everyone where I could find a good doctor, and they told me, 'In London there is a famous doctor,' and I immediately set out for London to bring the doctor here to you. But the doctor said to me, 'It is not necessary for me to go to the lion. I know what sickness your king has. I will tell you the treatment he needs and you advise him. This is the treatment: Cut in half a wolf—a very white wolf—and wrap your king with his hide. If you don't do that, the king will die.' I did not waste a moment of time and I returned immediately."

The wolf was still seated next to the lion. Quickly, the lion demanded that the wolf be slaughtered. The wolf's hide was wrapped around the lion. And the lion recovered from his sickness.

The lion cried, "Oh, what a worthless wolf! The fox did so much good for me and the wolf tried to harm her!"

THE MUSICIANS

Once upon a time a farmer in our village had a donkey. The donkey grew old. One day the farmer tied the donkey to a tree in the pasture and left him there to die. The farmer went home.

The old donkey was so sad. He hung his head and would not look up. He didn't even try to untie the rope.

Soon a hunter walked by with a hunting dog. But the hunter did not want the dog any longer. That hunting dog was just too old to catch rabbits. So the man walked away and left the dog alone.

The hunting dog saw the donkey tied up on the other side of the pasture. He walked over and asked, "What are you doing here, you poor old donkey?"

"My master tied me here because I am old," the donkey replied sadly.

"And my master left me here, too," the dog declared. "I can't hunt the rabbits anymore." He shrugged.

The donkey looked up. He suddenly had an idea and smiled brightly.

"How about coming with me and we'll become happy musicians?"

"I'll come!" replied the hunting dog.

The dog untied the donkey's rope and off they went.

Beyond the village, they saw a cat crying by a roadside. She rubbed her eyes with a handkerchief.

The old donkey asked, "Why are you crying, little friend?"

"Why am I crying?" the cat sobbed. Her eyes were very red from weeping. At last she looked up at the old donkey.

The cat cried, "I've grown old and I no longer can catch mice. My mistress chased me out of the house."

The old donkey comforted the cat. "Will you come with us? We're going to become musicians!"

"I'll come!" agreed the rooster with a smile. So he her tears.

The hunting dog then called out. "Old donkey, I can't walk. I'm too tired."

"Hop on my back," offered the donkey.

Up climbed the dog and then the cat. Off they rode, astride the donkey—clippety, clippety, clop—along the road.

On and on they traveled until they saw a country cottage. They noticed a rooster perched on a fence, wailing. The donkey asked him, "You poor old rooster, why are you crying?"

"Oh me, oh my," screeched the rooster, "my master has company for dinner and they're going to cook me."

"Oh! How about coming along with us?" asked the donkey. "We're going to become musicians!"

"I'll come." agreed the rooster with a smile. So he hopped on the donkey's back with the dog and cat.

As they rode on, the donkey, dog, cat, and rooster came to a forest. They decided to rest there overnight.

The donkey said, "Climb up a tall tree, old cat, and look around. See if you can find a lamp burning anywhere."

The cat climbed a stately cypress tree and looked around the forest. She saw a light shining from a little hut. The musicians went and found the hut. Inside, a band of robbers had gathered around the table.

At the very moment our musicians reached the hut, the robbers lowered the pot of food from the fire.

The old donkey put his head in the window and began braying loudly. *"Gka, gka, gkaouu . . ."*

"Ruuf, ruuf, ruuf, ruuuuuuf," sang the old dog.

"Ki-ki-ri-koooo, ki-ki-ri-kooooo ki-ki-ri-kooooooo," chimed the old rooster.

"Nia-ouoo, nia-ouoooo, nia-ouoooooo," the cat harmonized.

The robbers jumped up. "We're under attack," one robber cried, and they all ran away just as fast as they could.

But the old donkey and his party walked *into* the hut, sat down at the table, and ate and ate as much as they could.

When they had eaten every bit of food, the old donkey went outdoors and rolled contentedly in the grass. Old dog stretched out in the doorway. Old cat curled up on the warm hearth by the fire. And old rooster scrambled onto a bush in the garden.

At dusk, our musicians were sleeping peacefully.

Meanwhile, in another part of the forest, the captain of the robbers asked his troop, "Which of my brave men will run over to the hut and see what's happening?

"I will," offered one of the robbers.

"Go on then," commanded the captain.

When the robber reached the hut, the dog was resting quietly by the door.

The robber looked inside the hut and saw the cat's eyes shining from the hearth. He did not realize a cat was sitting there. He thought, "There's still some fire burning in the fireplace." So the robber moved closer to the hearth. He wanted some flame to light the wick of the oil lamp. When the robber bent down to light the wick, the old cat pounced on the robber's head.

The robber tried to escape. But the dog by the door grabbed the robber's leg. The robber pulled and pulled until he broke away.

Outside, the donkey began kicking the robber.

And from the tree, the rooster crowed, *"Ki-ki-ri-koooo, ki-ki-ri-koooooo,* catch him, catch him!"

"Gka, gka, gka, gkaouuu . . ." brayed the donkey.

"Ruuf, ruuf, ruuf, ruuuuuuf," sang the old dog.

"Nia-ouooo, nia-ouooooo, nia-ouoooo," harmonized the cat.

The robber ran away, panting, as fast as he could.

At last, he reached the captain and the band of robbers.

"What happened?" they asked, gathering around him.

"Oh me, oh my!" moaned the robber, rubbing his sores. "Forget that hut! I went to light the lamp and a witch in the fireplace grabbed my eyes. When I tried to run out the door, another one bit my legs.

Outside, a monster knocked me down and whacked me with a stick. And I heard loud screeching, "Catch him, catch him.'"

So the robbers never again stepped into the hut. And the old donkey, dog, cat, and rooster

Sang and ate without a fuss,
And never gave anything to us.

4

Our Hopes and Dreams

Ἡ ζωὴ εἶναι γλυκειά.

THE TWELVE MONTHS

ONCE UPON A TIME there was a poor woman called Zoe, a widow with five children. They lived in a small home at the edge of a forest. Zoe was so poor she did not have one drachma, and she could not find work to earn money to buy food for her children.

Every week, a wealthy neighbor asked Zoe to mix bread for her at her house. When the dough was mixed, the neighbor would not pay Zoe for her work. She would not even offer some of the dough as payment for the poor widow's trouble so that Zoe could bake her own bread. So poor Zoe hurried home to her youngsters with the dough stuck on her fingers.

When she arrived home, she washed her hands with clean water to make a paste from the dough, and she cooked it as a porridge for her children. With that meal, her children were satisfied until the wealthy neighbor called Zoe to knead more loaves. Again the poor mother returned home with some dough on her fingers, which she stirred in water to cook for her children's meal.

Now the children of the wealthy neighbor ate many kinds of rich foods and lavish dishes with the homemade bread that Zoe mixed. But they did not thrive. They looked like dried salt mackerels! Yet the poor widow's five children flourished. They were plump as fresh red snappers!

The wealthy woman was very upset. She complained to her friends.

The friends said, "The poor widow's children thrive because she takes your children's luck with her on her fingers! She goes home and feeds it to her children. That is why yours are so thin and hers are so healthy!"

The wealthy neighbor believed their words. When Zoe came once again to mix the bread, the wealthy neighbor would not allow her to take home any of the dough clinging to her fingers.

"*Wash your hands,*" she demanded. And poor Zoe had to remove every bit of dough from her hands. Then the poor mother returned to her children with tears in her eyes.

When the children saw their mother coming back without dough on her hands, they began to cry. The poor widow cried on this side of the room, and they cried on the other. At last, the mother, being older and stronger, summoned her courage, strengthened her heart like iron, and stood before her children.

"Courage, my children, don't cry. I will find a bit of bread for you."

Zoe went begging from door to door until someone at last gave her a crust of bread. She hurried home and soaked it for a long time in water. Then she divided it among her children. When they ate, she put them to bed, and they fell asleep. About midnight, she went out again because she could not bear to see her children dying of hunger.

The sky and path were pitch black as Zoe climbed

the rocky wilderness. Suddenly she noticed a tiny light flickering far away on a hill.

Zoe moved closer to the light until she observed a small tent. Looking inside a window, her attention was drawn to a large chandelier with twelve candles in the middle of the tent. Hanging from the chandelier was a round object shaped like a globe. When she stepped inside the tent, the poor widow perceived twelve youths discussing a serious matter that concerned them.

The tent was round. To the right of the entrance, three of the youths sat with their shirts unbuttoned and their chests bare. They held tender grasses and blossoms from fruit trees.

Beside them were three other youths holding sheaves of wheat. Their shirtsleeves were rolled up to their elbows.

Next came three other youths, holding large clusters of dark and golden grapes. The youths wore jackets with long sleeves.

Huddled together next to them sat the last three youths, wearing long fur coats that covered from their necks to their knees.

When they looked up and noticed Zoe, the youths smiled, "Welcome, auntie, be seated."

The poor widow greeted them and sat down. They asked how Zoe happened to visit them. She told them her troubles and of her search for work and food. When they were aware of her hunger, one youth who wore a fur coat stood up, brought her food and spread it before her. She noticed that he was lame.

71

After Zoe had eaten until she was full, the youths began asking her all kinds of questions about her village, and she answered them quietly.

Finally, a bare-chested youth asked, "Eh, auntie, how do you get along with the months of the year? What do you think of March, April, and May?"

"I get along well with them, my lads," replied the widow. "Certainly when these months come, the mountains and valleys turn green and the earth is dressed with many kinds of beautiful flowers and fruit trees. They bring such a sweet fragrance that everyone feels revived. The birds begin to sing and build new nests. Plowmen see their fields turn bright as emeralds and their hearts are glad as they prepare their storehouses. So we have no complaints of March, April, and May, or God will send fire and burn us for ingratitude."

Then the three youths with their sleeves rolled up, holding sheaves of wheat, asked, "Well, how about 'Harvester,' 'Thresher,' and August—how do they seem to you?"

And poor Zoe replied, "These months bring nothing that we would complain about because their warmth ripens the grains and fruits. The plowmen harvest their grains and the gardeners gather their fruits. Certainly the poor people are rewarded during those months, because they do not need much expensive clothing to keep warm."

Then she was queried by the three youths holding grapes. "How do you get along with September, October, and November, auntie?"

"During those months," responded the poor widow, "villagers gather their grapes and make wine. Another good feature, those months warn us that cold is coming. We gather wood and prepare heavy clothing to keep us warm during the winter."

Finally, the three youths wearing fur coats asked her, "Now, auntie, how do you get along with December, January, and February?"

"Ah, those months love us," smiled the poor widow, "and we love them! You will ask why! Here's why. Because folks are naturally greedy and like to work and work to keep earning more and more money. The winter months come along and gather us indoors to rest from the summer's work. We also love these months because the rains and snows nourish the grains and trees. So, my lads, all the months are good, each capable of doing a job that God commands. We the people are not good."

Then the youths beckoned the first youth holding grapes. He went out promptly and returned holding a sealed jug. He gave it to the widow and said, "Come now, auntie, take this jug and go to your home to live with your children."

Taking the jug gratefully, the woman said to them, "May you have many long and happy years, my lads."

"May your hours be good, auntie," they replied, and she departed.

Dawn was breaking as Zoe returned to her home. She found her children still asleep. Spreading a sheet on the table she emptied the jug and saw that it was full of gold coins! She was very happy.

As the sun rose and the day grew lighter, Zoe went to the *fourno* (village bakery) and bought five or six loaves of bread and went to the cheese store and bought one or so kilos of cheese.

Zoe woke her children, bathed them, made them say their prayers, and then she gave them bread and cheese. They ate until they were full.

Later, Zoe bought a kilo of wheat, took it to the mill to be ground and returned home to mix her dough. She took it to the bakery on a *pinakoti* (wooden board) to have it baked.

As Zoe was returning home carrying the bread board on her shoulders, the wealthy neighbor saw her and became curious. Hurrying to Zoe, she demanded: "Where did you find the flour to knead your bread?"

The kind widow told her everything, the full truth of all that had happened to her with the twelve youths.

The wealthy woman became very jealous! She decided that she would also go to find the youths. At night, when her husband and her children were asleep, she left home and followed the same road until she found the tent where the twelve youths were seated, and she greeted them.

They said to her, "Welcome, fine lady, how did you decide to condescend to visit us?"

"I am poor," she lied, "and I came so that you could help me."

"Very well, they said. "Are you hungry? Would you like something to eat?"

"No, thank you. I am quite full," she replied.

"Very well," said the youths. "How do you get along in your village?"

"May it not get worse!" she retorted.

"And how do you get along with the months?" they asked.

"How do we get along?" blared the rich woman. "Each month shows its wrath and fury. Just as we are getting accustomed to the heat of August, September rushes in, frenzied and hurried. October and November chill us, and some people catch pneumonia, others shiver.

"The winter months of December, January, and February come just to freeze us. The streets fill with snow and we can't go out. And that crippled February! . . . (Poor February heard that!)

"Then those stupid March, April, and May months come! Don't they know they are summer months instead of trying to pretend they are winter months, too, extending our winter for nine full months! Until the first of May, we cannot go out to drink our coffee with milk and to roll about in the grasses.

" 'Harvester' and 'Thresher' and August then arrive. They wish only to drown us in perspiration with their heat waves! In fact, after the hot spell of August 15, we are tormented with chills and coughing. Heavy winds tear the white clothes hanging on the lines. With those wretched months (may they be cursed!), we lead shattered lives!"

The youths said nothing, but nodded to the youth stooped over in the middle of the group, holding

75

wheat. He rose and brought a sealed jug, gave it to the wealthy woman and told her, "Take this jug, and when you are home, be sure to go at once into a room before you empty it. Do not open the jug on the way home."

"No, I won't open it," she promised. Full of anticipation, she arrived home before daybreak. She locked herself in a room, spread a sheet on the table and emptied the jug.

What did she find? Snakes! They pounced on her and ate her alive. Her children were orphaned because it is not good for one person to condemn another.

The poor widow Zoe, however, with her good heart and sweet words, lived a happy life. She taught her children how to behave and helped them.

POPPY

ONCE UPON A TIME an old woman had a young daughter. She would send her daughter to the field to pick wild greens for their dinner.

One sunny day in May, wildflowers were in bloom, shining with radiant colors—reds and pinks, blues and violets and exuberant yellows. Blossoms gleamed on the fruit trees and leaves were sprouting everywhere. The girl ran into the meadow. But instead of gathering herbs and greens, she began picking brilliant red poppies.

With the needle and thread she carried in her pocket, *matia mou*,[1] she began sewing the poppies to her dress.

As she adorned herself from the top of her waist to the hemline, the Three Fates walked by. When they saw her sewing the poppies on her dress, they paused and laughed. They all chuckled and giggled, including the youngest Fate who had never ever laughed!

"Ha, ha, ha! Look at the silly girl sewing poppies on her dress." The Three Fates decided to call the girl "Poppy."

"Since you made our sister merry enough to laugh,

[1]*Matia mou* ("my eyes") is an endearing expression that mothers and grandmothers in Greece often use when addressing their children.

Poppy, what can we wish for you?" asked the first Fate.

The Three Fates stood quietly and thought about their wish.

The first Fate expressed her wish. "May the poppies on your dress become rubies and diamonds."

The second Fate wished: "Poppy, may you become the most beautiful maiden in the world and when you speak, Poppy, may peaches and roses fall from your lips."

Then the third and youngest Fate spoke. "Poppy, who made me laugh. . . . Very soon the king will pass by. He will fall in love with you and take you to his palace to be his queen."

Poppy stood speechless. She was surprised by their wishes. Then she began to romp again among the flowers.

Very soon, *matia mou*, along comes the king, riding on his splendid white horse. Spread on the horse like a saddle was a white linen cloth embroidered with flowers and leaves.

When the king saw Poppy dancing about in the wildflowers with her dress all trimmed with fresh poppies, his eyes brightened. He was breathless. She was so beautiful.

"Are you a person or a fantasy?" he implored.

"A person," replied Poppy, laughing.

"Come here," the king said.

The king lifted Poppy onto the horse's back and rode off with her to his palace. He took Poppy to his mother.

When she saw Poppy, the Queen was amazed. "My son," she asked, "what is this? A marvel, a vision it is."

"No, my mother," answered the king. "Don't worry. Poppy is real."

So I'll tell you quickly what happened. The king was very much in love. He married Poppy. They lived very happily in the palace.

One day when they sat in their room and Poppy was combing his hair, she began to giggle. "Ha, ha, ha." She couldn't stop laughing.

"What is so funny?" the king demanded.

"Oh," answered Poppy between her giggles. "What can I tell you? Your beard reminds me of our palace broom! Ha, ha, ha."

The king was angry. "Oh, Poppy, how could you say such a thing!" he flared. "Do you think so little of me?"

He stormed out of the room and went straight to the Twelve Judges to ask what should be done. They told the king to have Poppy sentenced to death.

Meanwhile, the Three Fates who had blessed Poppy, perceived what happened and why the king was so enraged.

"My, oh my," cried the Fates. "Poppy is still doing foolish things! What will happen to her now! She will be harshly punished for her mindless words."

So they thought of a plan to save Poppy.

The Fates built three brilliant schooners and changed themselves into three fine captains. They sailed away and docked near the king's palace and began to shoot cannons!

The king's servants ran to the dock to see the ships with bright flags waving on the masts.

"Three kingly vessels! Three handsome ships have arrived," called the servants, blowing their trumpets.

The king, dressed in his finest robes, went to meet the visitors, according to the custom of his land. "Welcome to my kingdom," said he.

The Fates (disguised as captains) spoke to the king. "We learned that you have our sister, Poppy, whom we had lost."

"Yes," admitted the king. His face turned red with shame, remembering that the Twelve Judges had sentenced Poppy to death.

It was the custom in his kingdom to entertain visitors. So the king invited the three captains to the palace. Dinner was served.

After dinner, the visitors made a request: "We wish to see our sister."

Servants escorted the visitors to the queen's parlor. When they were alone, the visitors scolded Poppy.

"You silly girl, why did you say such thoughtless words to your husband? Isn't it enough that you have been made queen of the land and you have a good life? Did you have to insult your husband? Do you know that they have decided to punish you by putting you to death?"

When Poppy heard their reproaches, she knew they were the Three Fates in disguise—the same Fates who had blessed her. She was very happy to see them again. But she was also very upset to hear about her cruel sentence. Poppy burst into tears. She asked the

Fates what to do. What could be done to save her life?

"Because we are the Fates who blessed you when you made our youngest sister laugh, we will help you once again. Take this little broom decorated with diamonds and rubies. Hang it behind your door. When the king comes into the room and asks what it is, you reply, 'My king, this is what I meant when I laughed about your beard, because we have beautiful objects in our palace,' " the Three Fates advised. "Poppy, be thoughtful. Be kind. Next time, be very careful, not silly."

Poppy listened carefully. She thanked them and dried her eyes, promising to think before saying senseless words. They said goodbye.

The visitors stopped by the king's parlor to thank him for his hospitality. The king escorted the Three Fates to the dock and wished them a good voyage. The Fates boarded their schooners and sailed away.

The king returned to the palace and decided to visit Poppy once again. As he turned to close the door, he saw a sparkling object on the door. The little jeweled broom glittered on the door.

"What is this?" he asked.

Poppy replied gently. "It is what I meant is like your beard, because we have beautiful items in our palace."

The king was very happy to hear Poppy's words. He thought to himself, "Oh, it was unfair that I wanted to have my darling queen executed. She did not say words to degrade me. She wanted to honor me, and I misunderstood."

So he forgave Poppy. He truly loved her, and they lived happily ever after and we even better.

TRAK!

ONCE UPON A TIME there were three brothers. The family was so poor that the brothers had to leave our village to find work far away.

The brothers walked and walked. At last they came to a meadow at the edge of a pine forest. They saw a spring. So they paused to eat.

As they ate their bread, along came an old man, leaning on his cane. He had snowy white hair and wore dark pants and a sweater over his shirt. When he reached the brothers, he smiled.

"Good day to you, lads," greeted the old man.

"May you have many happy years, *Papou*,[1] they replied The youngest brother broke off a piece of his bread.

He said, "Join us, *Papou*. Here is some bread for you."

The old man sat down with the brothers and began eating small pieces of the bread.

As they ate, the old man and brothers heard noisy crows in the forest. "Caw, caw, caw."

The old man turned to the oldest brother and asked, "What would you wish for more than anything in the world, my son?"

[1]*Papou* means "grandpa" and in Greece is a respectful way of addressing old men.

The oldest brother replied very quickly, "I would like all those crows to become sheep and to be mine. Then I could be a shepherd."

"Good," responded the old man. "Sheep are gentle animals and give milk. But if some poor person came and asked you for a little milk, would you give some?"

"I would," promised the oldest brother, "I would offer milk or cheese, whatever they ask for."

Trak! The old man struck the earth with his cane and the crows became sheep! The green meadow turned white with sheep.

Up rose the oldest brother. He gathered his flocks and cared for the sheep at the edge of the forest.

The other two brothers and the old man said goodbye to the shepherd brother and continued on their journey. They walked and walked until they reached a hill covered with shrubs.

The old man asked the second brother, "What would you wish for more than anything in the world?"

"I would like, *Papou*, for all those woody shrubs to be olive trees and for them to be mine," he replied immediately.

"Good," said the old man. "Olive trees provide shade from the heat, olives and olive oil are good for food, and olive wood is strong to build homes. But if you had so many olive trees would you give some olive oil to poor people?"

"I would give," promised the second brother.

Trak! The old man struck the earth with his cane and the woody shrubs turned into olive trees full of ripe olives. The second brother opened a shop there, filled the barrels with olives and oil pressed from the remaining olives. He loaded the barrels on boats.

The youngest brother remained alone with the old man. They said goodbye to the second brother in his olive orchard and continued on their trip. Soon they reached a crossroad where there was a fresh spring. They sat by the well and splashed water on their faces to cool off.

The old man asked the youngest brother, "Well, won't you tell me your wish, too?"

The lad looked carefully at the spring. "*Papou*," he replied, I would like honey to flow from this spring."

"And would you give honey to the poor if they ask for some?" asked the old man.

"I would give," replied the youngest brother.

Trak! The old man struck the earth with his cane and at once, honey flowed from the spring. The old man said goodbye and continued on his journey.

The youngest brother stayed there and lived by the crossroad, selling honey and offering some to poor people who wandered by.

After a few years had passed, he missed his older brothers and wanted to visit them. He asked a worker to stay by the spring and offer honey and he set out to visit his brothers.

When he reached the hill where the olive trees had been, he saw only woody shrubs. He did not see his brother who had the olive orchard. He continued on the road, looking for sheep at the edge of the forest. But he only heard loud cawing from the crows perched on the pines. There were no sheep. He could not find his older brother who had become a shepherd.

As he stood there, wondering what had happened, he saw the old man coming toward him, leaning on his cane.

The old man greeted the youngest brother and said, "So now you see, my boy. Your brothers did not keep their promises. They did not share with the poor from the gifts I gave them. That is why I took back the olive trees and the sheep. You have remained faithful, and you have my blessing."

Trak! As he finished speaking, the old man struck the ground with his cane and disappeared.

TINA, THE UNLUCKY PRINCESS

ONCE UPON A TIME a queen had three daughters. But the queen could not find husbands for her princesses, and she was very, very troubled.

"Oh me, oh my," she moaned all day long, wringing her hands. The queen worried that her princesses would grow old and never be happily married with families of their own.

One day a beggar woman, who was also a fortune teller, visited the palace. She begged for food.

When she noticed the queen's unhappy face, the beggar asked what was wrong. The queen told the beggar woman about her fears.

The beggar said, "Listen to me, as I say. At night, when your daughters are asleep, go and look at them. Tell me in what positions they sleep!"

The queen went to their rooms and watched as the daughters slept. She noticed the oldest daughter fell asleep with her arms up over her head; the second daughter crossed her arms over her breast; and her youngest daughter, called Tina, slumbered with her hands crossed over her knees.

In the morning the queen related to the beggar the sleeping positions of her daughters.

"Your highness," declared the beggar. "Your daughter who sleeps with her arms crossed over her knees is the one with the unlucky fate! It is her bad luck that blocks the good luck of your other two daughters!"

When the beggar departed, the queen remained sad. "Oh me, oh my!" cried she. The queen still did not know what to do to help her princesses.

But Tina, her youngest daughter came to her mother and expressed herself, "Now let me say something, Mother. I heard you talking to the beggar woman. I understand that I stand in the way of both of my sisters' happiness. Give me all of my dowry in *floria*.[1] Sew the coins into the hem of my skirt and let me go away. Don't worry about me anymore, please."

"No, no," cried the queen. She did not want Tina to leave. "Where will you go, my child?"

But Tina would not change her mind. She disguised herself as a nun and said goodbye to her mother.

As she was leaving, two princely suitors arrived at the palace gate for her sisters.

So Tina, the unlucky princess, walked and walked. At dusk she reached a small village. At the door of a fabric shop, she asked if she could spend the night there.

The shopkeeper told Tina that she was welcome upstairs in his home with his family, but Tina declined. She said, "The shop will be just fine for me to rest, thank you."

That night, Tina's Fate went and damaged all the

[1]*Floria* are gold coins known as "florins" in other countries. Young women traditionally received a *proika* (dowry), comprised of handmade linens, weavings, and embroideries, and when the family was wealthy, gold and silver or animals and property were also given.

fabrics in the shop, ripping them into scraps. Tina begged her to stop. But the Fate wouldn't listen to Tina and made a mess on the shelves and floor. The Fate threatened to tear Tina into pieces, too!

The next morning the shopkeeper came down from his home upstairs to inquire how the nun had spent the night. But he was shocked to find all the fabrics torn in pieces, scattered around the shop.

The shopkeeper exclaimed "Oh, sister, you have destroyed me! What terrible damage you have done to me! What can I do?"

"Be still, wait," Tina replied. She turned up her hem and handed him some gold coins. "Will these be enough to cover the damages?"

"Enough? They are more than enough ..."

So they uttered farewells and Tina continued on her journey. She traveled for many days until she reached another country. At nightfall, Tina stopped to rest.

The same thing happened! Tina asked the owner of a glass shop if she could rest overnight in the shop. At night, her Fate came and broke every glass object on the shelves.

The next day, the shopkeeper returned to the shop to see how Tina had spent the night. He was very distressed by all the broken glass! He scolded Tina. But when Tina filled his hands with gold pieces, he stopped shouting and allowed her to leave.

So, Tina, the unlucky princess, still dressed as a nun, continued on her journey until she reached the palace of the king in another country. Tina asked to see the queen and indicated that she would like to work for her.

The queen was very intelligent. She realized that the young woman, dressed as a nun, actually was a wealthy princess in disguise. The queen asked Tina if she knew how to embroider with a pearl needle. Tina replied, indeed, she could embroider. So the queen gave Tina work to do.

But when Tina began to embroider, the portrait figures on the walls would come down from their frames and snatch the pearl needle and tease Tina. They would not give her a moment's peace!

The queen observed what happened and felt sorry for Tina. Frequently, the palace maids complained to the queen that all the dishes and glasses were broken and that Tina had broken them herself.

The queen declared to the maids, "You all be quiet. Tina is certainly a princess from a fine family. But she has an unlucky Fate, the poor dear."

Eventually, the queen said to Tina, "Listen to me, my child, you cannot live like this with your Fate always tormenting you. You must find a way to deal with your Fate to change your luck!"

"What shall I do?" asked Tina. "How can I get rid of my bad luck? How can I be blessed with good luck?"

"Come, let me tell you," explained the queen. "Do you see that high mountain far in the distance? Up there all the Fates of the world are gathered together. That is their palace and that is the road you must travel. Climb to the mountaintop and find your Fate.

Confront her. Give her this slice of bread and say, 'My Fate, you have given me bad luck. Please give me a new Fate.' *Tina, don't leave the mountain, no matter what your Fate says or does, until she takes the bread and holds it in her hand."*

This is exactly what Tina did. She took the bread and set out on the path until she reached the mountain peak. When she arrived at the palace, Tina knocked on the garden gate. A lovely Fate unlatched the gate, smiling at Tina. Her hair was well groomed and she wore a splendid blue dress. Soon another pleasant Fate appeared.

"We don't recognize you, my good maiden," the gracious Fates uttered, and strolled back into the garden.

Many charming Fates came, one after another, but they withdrew because they did not know Tina.

Then suddenly, one ragged weirdo appeared at the gate, scowling and shaking a stick threateningly. Her hair was unkempt. Her dress was tattered and torn. Her teeth were almost all missing.

"What do you want, you dreadful creature?" she shrieked at Tina. "Why did you come here? Go away. I'm going to kill you!"

Poor Tina realized this untidy wretch was *her Fate.* Tina kept trying to give her the bread, pleading, "My Fate, you have given me such bad luck. Please change my luck! Help me! Change my luck! Give me good luck!"

"Oh, go get lost!" sneered the nasty Fate, taunting Tina. "Go tell your mother to give birth to you all over again, to nurse you again, and then come back and I'll change your luck!"

But Tina would not leave. The amiable Fates attempted to help Tina. They beseeched the bad Fate, "Change the luck of this unhappy maiden who is really a good person. *Change her luck!*"

"No! Send her away!" screeched Tina's Fate stubbornly.

Suddenly the bad Fate grabbed the bread from Tina's hand and threw it at her, and then stumbled and fell.

Tina picked up the bread and thrust it again toward the Fate's hand, repeating fervently, "Take this bread, my Fate, take it and change my luck." But the Fate kept chasing Tina away, jeering and throwing sticks and stones.

Well, at last, with all the Fates urging the bad Fate, and Tina pleading with her to accept the bread, the bad Fate finally relented.

"Give it to me," howled the bad Fate, snatching the bread.

Tina stood trembling, afraid that the Fate would again throw it at her.

But the Fate held the bread in her hand and cried, "Listen to me! Take this spool," and she tossed a large spool of silk thread to Tina. "Be careful. Don't sell it and don't lose it, but give it only to someone who asks for it by its true weight. Go now and do what you must do."

Tina seized the spool and returned to the queen. Now Tina always kept the spool with her. She was not bothered by the Fate or the portrait figures or anyone!

Meanwhile, in a neighboring country, the kingdom was preparing for the king's wedding. But more silk thread was needed for the bridal gown. The silk had to match exactly. . . .

Therefore, the king's servants requested matching silk for the bridal gown from anyone who had silk.

The servants had heard a report that in a nearby palace, a maiden had a spool of silk thread. So they went and found Tina and asked her to come with them to the king's palace to see if her silk thread matched the color of the gown.

When they arrived there, they held Tina's silk thread near the bridal gown and found that it matched perfectly! The servants asked Tina how much money she wanted for the silk. They needed to buy it. Tina said that she would sell it only by its true weight.

So the servants placed the silk spool on one side of a balance scale and gold coins on the other side of the scale. They kept adding more gold coins but the scale would not move!

Then the prince came and stood on the scale and the prince weighed the same as the spool of thread! The prince smiled. He declared to Tina, "Since your silk and I are the same weight, we can have your silk only if you will marry me."

That it exactly how it happened. Tina married the prince. They had a fine wedding and lived happily ever after and we even better.

THE ALMOND-PASTE PRINCE

ONCE UPON A TIME in a glorious kingdom far from our village, a youthful princess lived with her parents in a fine castle. Her name was Thalia and she was very vivacious.

Thalia liked to sing and dance and play the harp. Her father, the king, wanted her to marry a young prince and invited many suitors to meet her. But Thalia was not interested in any of them because she had never fallen in love. So she decided to make a man for herself.

Thalia asked her father, "Please bring me a sack of almonds, a sack of semolina, and a sack of sugar."

Her father brought her the almonds, semolina, and sugar.

Thalia declared, "I must stay in this room for forty nights and forty days. Do not ask me to come out until then." So she locked herself in her room.

Alone, she cracked the almonds and ground them. Then she mixed the almonds with the semolina and sugar and kneaded them together to make a soft almond paste. Thalia carefully molded the almond paste into the shape of a man.

Then she began her prayers, burning incense and whispering, "Speak to me, my darling, won't you speak to me, my joy?" Holding him gently, she pleaded and wept for forty days until on the fortieth day, he opened his eyes and looked at her.

"Ah, how sweetly I was sleeping and you woke me up!" said he.

The princess laughed and hugged him, drying her tears. She danced excitedly around the room and joyfully ran to open the door. She sang a melody of love and led the Almond-Paste Prince to meet the king and queen.

"Here," she declared to her father, "here is the man I want to marry."

Her parents looked at the Almond-Paste Prince. He was tall and pleasant. When he smiled, his eyes sparkled.

The king and queen prepared for the splendid occasion, the wedding of the princess Thalia to the Almond-Paste Prince. Special clothes were designed and invitations were sent out. The entire kingdom feasted and danced in celebration of their marriage.

The happy news spread throughout the land as far away as a distant kingdom where the king and queen had a very jealous daughter. When she heard about the wedding, the jealous princess put on her black clothes and cried, "I'm going to die unless you bring the Almond-Paste Prince to me. I want him for myself!"

"But how can we do that?" asked her parents. "He belongs to the princess who made him and married him." Their daughter whined and wailed with many tantrums. Her parents were distressed by her actions and were afraid that she would become very sick.

The king and queen of the distant kingdom made a plan. "Let us build a golden ship with golden oars and fill it with jewels and fine crystal. We will then capture the Almond-Paste Prince."

When the golden ship was ready, the king said to the captain, "Go to the kingdom where the Almond-Paste Prince lives. Dock near the palace and as soon as he comes on board, set sail immediately and bring him to me."

So the golden ship sailed away to the kingdom where Thalia lived with her prince and docked near the palace. When the palace servants heard about the golden ship, they went to Thalia and told her, "Ah, my lady, a great ship has arrived with many beautiful objects. Everyone is going on board to buy gold and silver and emeralds."

"Won't you go, my dear Almond-Paste Prince, and buy something for me?" asked Thalia.

"But, why?" he countered. "We have everything we need."

But Princess Thalia convinced him to go to the ship and, of course, the queen's sailors recognized him immediately because of his handsome appearance! They captured him and set sail!

In the evening, Thalia waited and waited, but her prince did not return. She asked here and there and someone told her, "He was captured and sailed away on the golden ship."

She cried and cried. What would she do without her Almond-Paste Prince? She was very unhappy.

Then she dried her tears and resolved to find him.

She made three pairs of little iron shoes and put on a pair and took the first road she could find. She traveled here and there, to this place and that place, searching everywhere until she found the moon's mother.

"Good hour to you, blessed mother," greeted Thalia.

"Welcome to the lady. What are you doing on this planet?"

"My fate has brought me," replied Thalia sadly. "Mother of the moon, have you seen the Almond-Paste Prince?"

"Where, my dear? I hear that name for the first time. But wait until my child who circles the earth returns tonight. He may have seen him somewhere."

That evening when the moon came home, his mother asked, "My child, this princess asks you please, have you seen the Almond-Paste Prince?"

"Where? I did not see him. I hear that name for the first time. You must go to the sun. The sun could have seen him because he travels farther."

That night Thalia slept at the moon's house, and in the morning they gave her an almond and told her, "If you should have trouble and need help, crack this almond."

Thalia thanked them and took the almond and continued her search.

She traveled far and wide to this place and to that place and wore out one pair of little iron shoes until she found the sun's mother. She repeated the same questions and the mother could not help her, but asked her to wait and ask the sun. The sun had not seen the Almond-Paste Prince either but told Thalia to go ask the many stars. So Thalia rested and in the morning, the sun gave her a walnut to crack if she should need help.

She traveled far and wide and wore out another pair of little iron shoes until she found the stars' mother and the stars.

"No, we have not seen him," the stars chimed.

Then a very tiny star cried out, "I saw him!"

The princess was so happy! "Where did you see him, tiny star?" she asked.

"In a small white house near the palace there are little geese. This is where the queen keeps the Almond-Paste Prince captive so that no one will come and take him away.

That night the princess slept there and in the morning before she left, they gave her a filbert to crack if she had trouble.

Thalia traveled for many days until she found the palace where the Almond-Paste Prince was kept captive. Thalia dressed herself as a beggar. When she went closer, she saw the Almond-Paste Prince but said nothing. She had to find a way to take him home again.

She went to the servants and asked, "Won't you let me stay where you keep the geese?"

The servants asked the queen, "Your highness, there is a beggar outside asking if she can stay with the geese. What shall we tell her?"

"She may stay there," replied the queen.

Thalia slept in the goose barn that night. In the

morning when she awoke, she cracked the almond and out came a golden wheel spinning golden thread. The servants saw her spinning the golden thread and ran to tell the queen.

When the queen heard about the golden thread, she demanded, "Won't you go ask the beggar to give the golden spinning wheel to us. What could she possibly want with it?"

So the servants ran to ask the princess if she could have the golden spinning wheel with the golden reel.

"I'll give it to you only if you let me have the Almond-Paste Prince for one night," said Thalia.

The servants ran to ask the queen and she replied, "And why not give him? What will happen to him?"

After dinner that night, the queen gave the Almond-Paste Prince a sleeping potion and he fell asleep. The servants carried him to the beggar and took the golden spinning wheel to the queen.

When the servants left, Thalia began to speak and tried to awaken the Almond-Paste Prince "Won't you wake up, my darling? I'm the one who made you! The one who pounded almonds and sugar and semolina and shaped you! Aren't I the one who wore our three pairs of little iron shoes to find you and you won't even speak to me now? Don't you care about me, my dearest? Wake up!"

All night long, she tried to arouse him but could not make him open his eyes.

In the morning when the servants carried him away, the queen gave him another drink to wake him up.

Meanwhile, Thalia was very troubled, and she cracked the walnut. Out came a golden hen with golden chicks. The servants saw the golden hen and chicks and ran to the queen.

The same thing happened because the queen wanted the hen and chicks, too. And Thalia would not give them unless she could have the Almond-Paste Prince for the night. The queen agreed and again gave him a sleeping potion to drink.

All night long Thalia again cried, "Please, wake up, darling Almond-Paste Prince."

The next day the servants took him back to the palace. Thalia cracked the filbert. Out came a lovely carnation tree with golden carnations. The servants were amazed and ran to report it to the queen. Of course, the queen wanted the carnation tree, too, and once again loaned the Almond-Paste Prince for the night.

Meanwhile, next to the goose barn where the princess stayed, a tailor sat sewing every night. He heard all the crying and how Thalia tried to awaken the Almond-Paste Prince. So he secretly went to the Almond-Paste Prince and asked, "My prince, will you excuse me, may I ask a question?"

"You may," replied the Almond-Paste Prince.

"At night, where do you sleep?"

"Why do you ask? Here in the palace, of course! Where would I sleep?"

"Almond-Paste Prince, for two nights, I have not been able to close my eyes after work because of the beggar you have in the goose barn. All night long she cried, 'Almond-Paste Prince, why don't you wake up? I wore out three pairs of little iron shoes to find you and now you won't awaken.' "

The Almond-Paste Prince understood what happened but said nothing.

He went and prepared his horse with a saddlebag full of gold coins.

When the queen gave him a sleeping potion that night after dinner, he did not drink it but he pretended to fall asleep. The servants carried him to the beggar and took the carnation tree with the golden carnations.

As soon as they left, Thalia began speaking to the Almond-Paste Prince. He stood up and kissed her. They mounted the horse and rode away.

Imagine their surprise in the morning when the servants went to get the Almond-Paste Prince. They couldn't find him anywhere. What could the princess do?

"I'll make a man, too," she declared. She commanded her servants to crack some almonds, mixed them with sugar and semolina and made a man. But instead of praying, she cursed and cursed, and in exactly forty days the man became moldy and they threw him away. Now it was the selfish princess' turn to cry.

But Thalia and the Almond-Paste Prince escaped to their palace and lived happily ever after and we even better. I took a little walk there and I know.

BIBLIOGRAPHY

Aesop. *Aesop's Fables*. New York: Grosset & Dunlap, Inc., 1947.

Andersen, Hans Christian. *Andersen's Fairy Tales*, trans. Mrs. E. V. Lucas and Mrs. H. B. Pauli. New York: Grosset & Dunlap, 1945.

Aarne-Thompson, Stith. *The Types of Folktale: A Classification and Bibliography*. Helsinki, 1961.

Brown, Demetra V. and Phoutrides, Aristides, tr. *Modern Greek Stories*. Reprint of 1920 ed.

Dawkins, Richard M., ed. and tr. *More Greek Folktales*. Reprint of 1955 ed., 1974.

Gianakoulis, Theodore P. and Georgia H. MacPherson. *Fairy Tales of Modern Greece*. New York: Dutton, 1930.

Graves, Robert. *The Greek Myths*. New York: Penguin Books, 1966.

Halliday, William R. *Greek and Roman Folklore*. Reprint of 1930 ed. New York: Cooper Square.

Hamilton, Edith. *Mythology*. New York: New American Library, 1942.

Haviland, Virginia. *Favorite Fairy Tales Told in Greece*. Boston: Little, Brown, 1970.

Imam, Syed M. *Folklore of Ancient Greece*. New Jersey: Orient Books Distributor, 1976.

Ioannou, Georgos. *Paramythia tou Laou Mas* (Tales of Our People). Athens, Greece: Hermes, 1975.

Kyriakidis, Stilpon P. *Elliniki Laografia*, Athens, Greece, 1965.

Lawson, John C. *Modern Greek Folklore and Ancient Greek Religion: A Study in Survivals.*

Maury, Jean West. *Old Raven's World.* Boston: Little, Brown, 1931.

Megas, George A. *Ellinika Paramythia—A* (Greek Tales). Athens, Greece: Ioannou D. Kollarou & Sias, A.E., 1962.

Megas, George A. *Ellinika Paramythia—B* (Greek Tales, Vol. B). Athens, Greece: Estias, 1971.

Megas, George A. *Greek Calendar Customs.* Athens: Press and Information Dept., Prime Minister's Office, 1958.

Sanders, Irwin. *Rainbow in the Rock.* Princeton University Press, 1952. Sunnyvale, California. Folkloric Studies TGB Press, 1985.

Venizelou, I. *Paroimiai tou Ellinikou Laou* (Proverbs of the Greek People). Athens, Greece: Foititiki Gonia, 1965.